To My Wife, Emily, and Our Children:
Janice, Susan, Judith, and Howard.

—

DEVELOPING AN
OFFENSIVE
ATTACK
IN
BASKETBALL

● DEVELOPING AN OFFENSIVE ATTACK IN BASKETBALL

STAN WATTS

Englewood Cliffs, N. J.   PRENTICE-HALL, INC.

PRINTED IN THE UNITED STATES OF AMERICA

20485

Acknowledgements

Grateful acknowledgement is made to Dr. Edward L. Christensen and Miss Beverly Ann Painter for their help in preparing this book.

Acknowledgement is also made to the many fine men whom I have had the pleasure to be associated with during my coaching experiences.

Table of Contents

----

ix

1. Developing Variations in Your Offensive Attack (Cont.)

ZONE ATTACK WITH VARIATIONS *(Cont.)*

2. How to Select the Best Offensive Attack . . . 54

DEVELOPING AN OFFENSIVE ATTACK IN BASKETBALL

• 1 •

Developing Variations in Your Offensive Attack

A sound offensive attack in basketball is like a good watch: it has fine working parts. Unless the units work together in balance, precision, accuracy and rhythm, the whole will not function satisfactorily. The watchmaker uses time as his standard—the seconds gained or lost. As a basketball coach, your success is measured by games won or lost.

What Makes a Winning Attack?

Thus in developing a winning basketball attack, you cannot afford to neglect either the part or the whole method of coaching. It's like the proverbial chain which is strong as long as each link is strong. Because each opponent will do everything in his power to capitalize on your weakness, your team is both as strong and as weak as its weakest component.

Basketball is a game of skills blended into a working unit. Individual skills must contribute to team versatility. When a single part becomes more important than the whole, a team cannot enjoy uninterrupted success. All five men, and the replacing substitutes, must always put team success ahead of individual success. With

1

such a feeling of unity and cooperation, plus skillful execution of fundamentals and techniques, your team will more often taste the sweetness of victory.

Your Offense Should Have Several Variations

A number of offensive attacks are operating successfully today in both high school and college basketball. Granted, the high school coach has little or no opportunity to proselyte and must accept the material on hand, adjusting his system somewhat each year to meet the needs of his personnel. The college coach, on the other hand, solicits the type of player best adapted to his system. On either level, you cannot afford to sit still. You must be equipped to teach offensive variations, for the day (or more precisely the game) will come when this readiness will be a god-send.

Two Musts for Every Offense

To achieve a well balanced offense, your team must:

1. Be able to go quickly when an opportunity for outnumbered advantage presents itself.
2. Have an effective set attack when the defense recovers before your offensive attack materializes.

Let's look at the fundamentals and strategies for various systems of attack.

DEVELOPING THE FAST BREAK

The fast break, with its speed and fire, delights both the players and fans. With the threat of the fast break, you can always keep the defense a little more honest and prevent an opponent's ganging the boards or pressing you. Though speed is essential for such an attack, the main prerequisite is good, tough rebounding. In short, you must get the ball before you can run with it. Along with the missed-shot opportunity, the fast break presents itself off a bad pass, stealing a ball, free throws, and out-of-bounds situations. The fast break usually forms with a three-on-two or a two-on-one advantage where lanes are established and execution is good to capitalize on the advantage before the defense can recover.

The Fast Break Must Be Organized

Unless each man in the attack knows and carries out his responsibility, the fast break is wasted. Many times the three-lane attack is not spread sufficiently, so that the defense spreads with it. If two men are coming down the floor who are closer than approximately 15 feet, then one defensive man will be able to defense both of them.

At other times, a fast break is unsuccessful because the speed is not checked. Speed is very necessary after the first pass out, but as the attack nears the free throw area, the tempo must be slowed to allow successful completion of the play. The middle man on a three-on-two situation must make the defense commit and come out to force the play. The dribble will force the defense out quicker than the cross pass. When the side man in the attack attempts the dribble, the defense can delay commitment longer. The defensive man off the ball can drop back and defense the opposite wing man as well as the middle man.

All Men Should Know Responsibilities

All five men must know the attack well and function off the board in any position. More and more teams are taking the small man into the board area on certain plays or options. If your man doesn't know his assignment inside as well as outside, the attack may be slowed down; consequently each member of your team should be able to pass and dribble effectively. Various options in your attack should be practiced to compensate for the attempt on the part of the defense to stop your fast break.

Nowadays, most teams, in their offensive patterns, attempt to have two men back on each option. This semi-defensive balance is used to stop the fast break. Some teams send extra men to rebound offensively. Other teams attempt to slow the outlet pass or jam the receiving area of the first pass out. Every team must be aware of the many possibilities and know what to do to adjust to the defensive attempts to slow the fast break. Many times the defense will be keyed to stop the fast break. Your team will not have many opportunities to capitalize on the situation when this occurs. You should, however, always have this fast break threat in your attack. The defense will then be forced to play position and will not be able to take chances and crowd areas or double team your personnel. By keeping the defense worried and balanced, they are kept honest in their play and not allowed an advantage.

Making the Fast Break Work

Basic principles must be taught for effective fast break basketball. As previously mentioned, good rebounding is the key to the attack. Good ball hawking and tight defensive play will cause your opponents to make mistakes that may result in easy scores. Good passing and dribbling are essential. The baseball pass as well as the two-hand chest pass and the bounce pass must be executed well. Position in the two- or three-lane attack is important to maintain balance and keep the defense spread. The organization and tempo of the attack also become important parts in fast break basketball.

Consider the three-on-two fast break opportunity shown in Figure 1: Your opponent attempts and misses a shot. Immediately players 1, 2, and 3 set the defensive triangle in front of the bank-board, with players 4 and 5 in front ready to go. You take the rebound. If the outlet pass is made before the rebounder comes down to the floor, the fast break will hit quicker. Otherwise, the rebounder must alight and pass to player 5, who has assumed good position to receive the pass. The middle position of the three-lane attack may be filled by number 4. As this player occupies the middle position, he is ready to receive the second pass of the attack.

The other position on the wing or the opposite outside lane has been filled by number 3 coming off the triangle. The pass is made from 5 to 4, and 4 dribbles fast down the middle to force the defense to commit by coming out to stop the dribbler. Players 3 and 5 try to keep in line with 4, so as to be able to cut toward the basket from the side, receive the pass and make the shot attempt.

You must use caution not to have these men unbalanced so one is in advance of the other. If this occurs, your timing will be poor and the defense will gain an advantage.

Watch the Defense

The defense may be playing a two-man zone is front of the basket or a tandem defense. The tandem defense generally places one man at the freethrow line. The other man is directly behind him and in front of the basket. If the defense is in a zone, you will be able to get a shot at the foul line, since they will not come out to stop the middle man. In the event the defense is in a tandem, the front man's responsibility is to slow the dribbler. When he plays the dribbler, the other defensive man is forced to defense the two wing men moving toward the basket. After the pass is made to the wing man, the front defensive man will drop back opposite the pass to cover the other wing man. The center man in the three-lane attack should then be open for a pass and the shot. The center man must always stop at the free throw line to allow an opening by forcing the defense to play the wing men. Of course, if the defense will allow the center man to go all the way to the basket on his dribble, that becomes desirable but not probable.

The Trailer May Be Free

In case the defense recovers sufficiently to match the offensive attack with equal numbers, the trailer man may break free for a basket. The trailer is generally the fourth man down the floor on the fast break three-on-two situation. The trailer may be ahead of his defensive man to receive a short pass from the middle dribbler. The middle dribbler has to veer to his left or right approximately 10 feet in order to pull his defensive man with him. As the dribbler does this, it opens a path without opposition and allows his trailer teammate to go all the way or force an opponent to switch. When the switch takes place, another area will open. Generally, the rebounder passing the ball out will become the "safety valve" and does not go past mid-court. If there is an interception or a stolen ball taken by the defense, the safety man may be able to slow the opposition as it returns on the offensive attack.

A Two-on-One Situation

When the offensive team gains a two-on-one advantage, the attacking procedure will be about the same as the three-on-two situation. However, the two men attacking would split the floor distance to be in position to attack the one defensive man. In most cases, this position for each man will be halfway between the center of the floor and the sideline. If a gain of direction were to be made, it would be toward the middle of the floor and not to the sideline. The attacking dribbler must go as far as he can and attempt to force the defensive man to play him. Many times the defense will drop off on a fake pass, which allows the dribbler to go all the way. The defense may zone to force the long shot or to play the offensive man after he takes off for his shot. When this occurs, the man with the ball can make a flip pass to his teammate. When the defender goes into the air to block the driving layup, he creates the opening for the other offensive man.

A Two-on-Two Situation

In this pattern, many players on the offense will cross screen to evade the defense. In case the defense is playing tight, one of them may be screened. If the defense switches, the fast cut-away or the roll-off is possible. When the defense loosens to go through, the offensive man can shoot over the screen set by his teammate.

Fast Break Off the Free Throw

The fast break possibility is always present on the free throw attempt. If the free throw is made or missed, quick passing and the forming of attack lanes may result in an easy score. This pattern can be formed quickly and with the same organized plan as other fast break attempts.

Out of Bounds Situations

Quickness in getting the ball inbounds and down the floor with a long pass will catch the defense napping. This alertness will allow you to score some quick, cheap points. The baseball pass becomes an important factor in this development.

Teaching the Fast Break

The fast break attack cannot be taught and perfected overnight; many hours of practice time must be utilized. The team must always be fast break conscious and know when the opportunity is there. The team members must be able to recognize the opportunity in your scrimmages and games.

When teaching this type of attack, start from the beginning and make the instructions simple but exact.* Practice the fast break off the defensive board most of the time. This situation will present most the opportunitties to go quickly. The objective of the fast break and the proper execution of it should be explained thoroughly on the blackboard. Floor practice can then follow the chalked explanation. Running the pattern off the rebound opportunity at half speed with no opposition should begin the instruction. After the team members can operate the fast break patterns well without opposition, place defensive men on the rebounding triangle to make the offense protect their position on the board. Situate other defensive men at mid-court to pick up the first wave of the offense. By placing two men at mid-court or closer, the game situation is presented.

After two or three days, the defensive men can vary their movements to acquaint the offensive team with various possibilities. By varying action defensively you may observe and make corrections and adjustments that the team is unable to do at this early stage of practice. Full court drill, with and without opposition, is also a good conditioning drill, as it allows for running as well as practice on fundamentals.

Half court three-on-two and two-on-one drills must also be practiced to get the operation in the front court attack. These drills help to adjust the tempo of the attack and check the floor position of the men. The full court drill must be coordinated with the half court drill for more effective results off the fast break.

* For a detailed treatment of the fundamentals of teaching the fast break, see *How to Coach Fast Break Basketball,* by Michael Esposito (Englewood Cliffs, N. J.: Prentice-Hall, Inc., 1959).

Fast Break Responsibilities and Execution of Opportunities

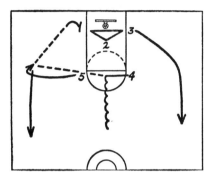

Fig. 1.

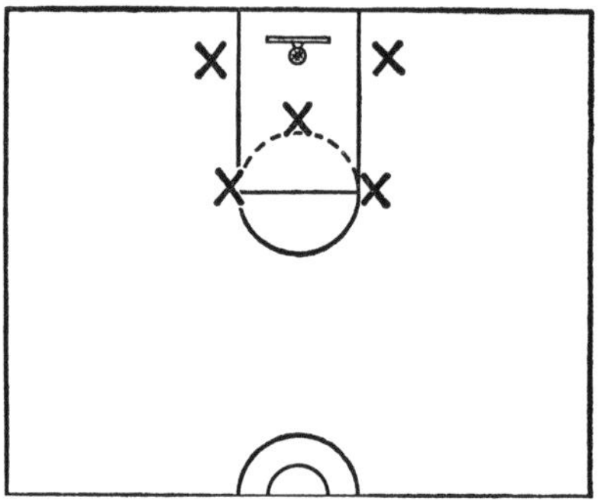

Fig. 1A. General position on rebounding situation for fast break.

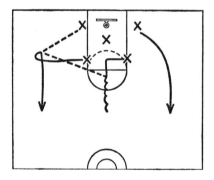

Fig. 2. Fast break pattern on outlet pass, side man rebounding.

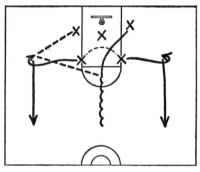

Fig. 3. Fast break pattern on outlet pass, side man rebounding.

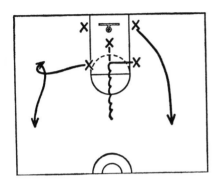

Fig. 4. Fast break pattern on outlet pass, center man rebounding.

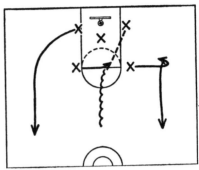

Fig. 5. Fast break pattern on outlet pass, side man rebounding.

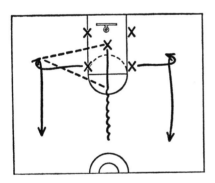

Fig. 6. Fast break pattern on outlet pass, front man rebounding.

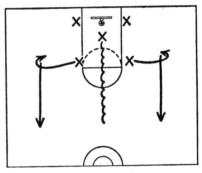

Fig. 7. Fast break pattern on outlet dribble of front rebounder.

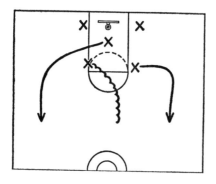

Fig. 8. Fast break pattern on long rebound to front men.

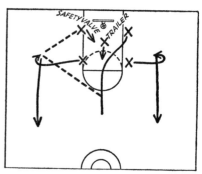

Fig. 9. Trailer and safety valve responsibilities on side rebound.

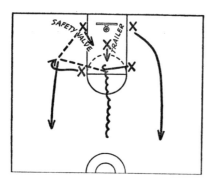

Fig. 10. Trailer and safety valve responsibilities on side rebound.

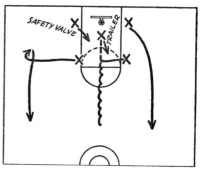

Fig. 11. Trailer and safety responsibilities on front rebound.

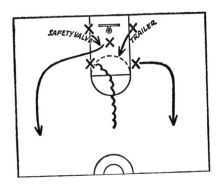

Fig. 12. Trailer and safety valve responsibilities on long rebound.

Front Court Attack on Fast Break

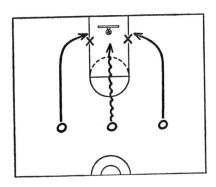

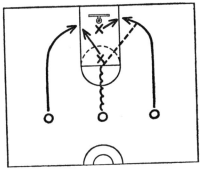

Fig. 13. 3-on-2 attack against zone-type defense. Middle man should go all the way if possible.

Fig. 14. 3-on-2 attack against tandem-type defense. Middle man should stop at free throw line for return pass.

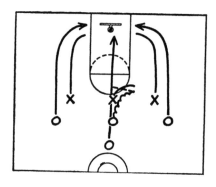

Fig. 15. Trailer opportunity on 3-on-3 situation.

Fig. 16. 2-on-1 attack. Dribbler must force defensive man to commit himself.

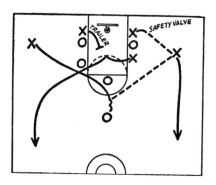

Fig. 17. Fast break following missed free throw from the heavy side.

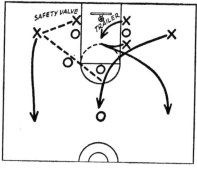

Fig. 18. Fast break following missed free throw from the light side.

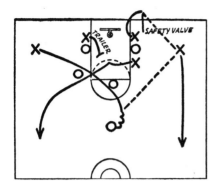

Fig. 19. Fast break following successful free throw from the heavy side.

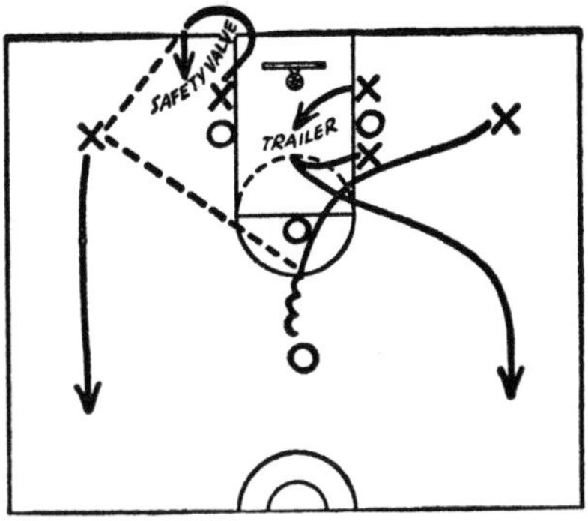

Fig. 20. Fast break following successful free throw from the light side.

Fast Break Drills

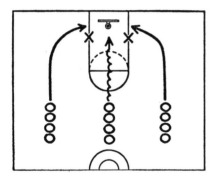

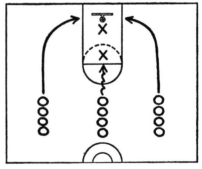

Fig. 21. 3-on-2 half-court drill against zone.

Fig. 22. 3-on-2 half-court drill against tandem.

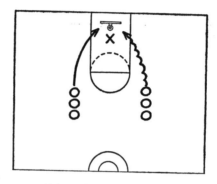

Fig. 23. 2-on-1 half-court drill.

YOU WILL NEED A STRONG SET ATTACK

When your fast break attempt is stopped, your team should have a good set attack to rely on. Your set attack must have good floor balance and a minimum number of plays and options. Again the philosophy of doing a few things well takes precedence over doing many things adequately. You should also consider simplicity of attack and keep plays and options at a minimum. The number must not be too few, however, to inform the defense what is coming. Minimum numbers of plays and options will allow the players to know, and know well, what the strategic plan is. Repetition of drills and patterns will train them thoroughly and in detail to know what to do.

There are many stories about coaches who attempt to teach as many as 30 or 40 basic plays. When options vary from one to four for each play, it becomes impossible to perfect this number of plays. Of course, each of a few basic plays will have approximately four options to counter any move of the defense. Good teams must have several series of patterns to operate efficiently. A series of four or five plays, with options, should be sufficient along with a zone attack, an attack for a press, and a control game.

Do not stereotype your set attack and make the player "machine like" in his patterns. If you do, unorthodox defensive procedures will result, making it difficult to effect your patterns. Too few options will enable a good defensive team to stymie your attack.

Screens Should Be Used

When competition becomes keener each year and the player abilities improve, the possibility of beating an opponent on a one-on-one situation is less apt to occur. If your offensive player gets by his opponent, other defensive men will pick him up to stop his attempt at the basket. Thus the players must be taught proper screening techniques for set attack patterns. The most popular screens are single moving screens which create an opening inside or outside. Some teams prefer set screens to the moving screens, whereas some teams use both types of screens. Mass screens used by some teams, if effective, cause headaches for the defense. These screens consist of setting two or three men together which enables the shooter to come off the screen and obtain a good set shot.

There is always the chance for illegal screening to exist if you do not explain and differentiate between the proper and improper way to screen. The rule states you must set far enough from the opponent to allow movement without contact. Especially in intersectional games, take care to avoid illegal screening. Though different interpretations of legal and illegal screening exist in various sections of the country, your team will fare well if it sets a screen far enough from the opponent to allow movement without contact. Fouls will be called if your squad sets too close to the opponent and restricts his movement.

Inside and Outside Needs

To work properly, a set attack must consist of a good inside attack and a good outside attack. Most teams operate the inside attack with a screening and driving game. The outside attack becomes successful with screening and good shooting over the screens. When a team has players that can screen, drive, and shoot, it can keep a defense loose. You must be able to get inside the defense to get the good percentage shot. When you accomplish this attack, many defenses will jam the lanes to such an extent that your driving and screening game is stopped. You then must be able to draw this tight defense out with screens and good shots over the screens. To outscore your opponent, your offensive moves must create openings for the good shot.

Of course, follow-up is necessary to get the good second shot when the first one fails. Proper rebounding and defensive balance become part of this attack. Along with screening, cutting and driving techniques are needed. Such techniques as angle cuts, L cuts, scissor cuts and others may be used successfully. Angle cuts are set up by taking a direction with a sharp angle change up. These angles can vary in degree according to the players' position on the floor. L cuts are about the same as angle cuts, with the exception that the L cut change up is a direct right angle change. Scissor cuts consist of using a post man to run the opponent into a screen. A double scissor cut occurs when two men split the post to come off the screen set by the post man. Some coaches refer to these maneuvers as ruboffs, since the man is purposely taken into the screen from his blind side.

There are many types of set attacks used in present-day basketball. These types will be discussed in a later chapter. For purposes of illustration, to show balance and floor position, a single post set attack is diagrammed.

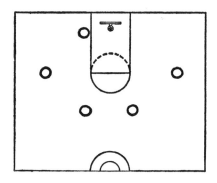

Fig. 24. Single post attack with
center off ball.

Screens are illustrated to show the various types and execution of techniques.

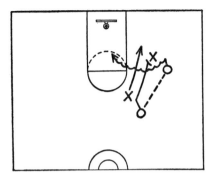 

Fig. 25. Inside screen.   Fig. 26. Outside screen.

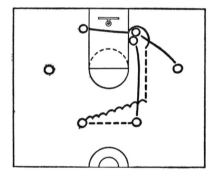

Fig. 27. Double screen.

The inside and outside attack options demonstrate the need for such attacks for balanced offensive power. (See Figs 28-31 on page 18.)

SEMI-CONTROL GAME

Many situations during the game demand a change of plans, or an altering of the attack. When a team has built a lead into the third or fourth quarter, strategy will be needed to protect the lead.

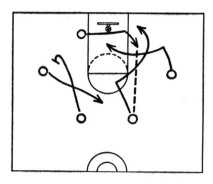

Fig. 28. Inside attack option—split post.

Fig. 29. Inside attack option—open center.

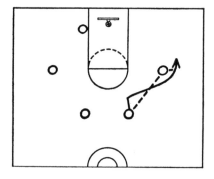

Fig. 30. Outside attack option—single post.

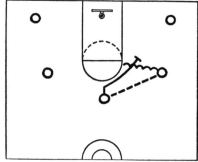

Fig. 31. Outside attack option—open center.

A change of attack will be necessary for a possessive offense with only the high percentage shot attempted. In this strategy, however, your team must not stop its attempt to score, and pressure on the defense must be maintained. The mentioned situation becomes a semi-delayed attack with emphasis stressed to protect a lead. Take special care to minimize mistakes and do not attempt long shots.

During this type of semi-delayed game, there is no need to change the style of the set attack. The emphasis must be placed, however, on the inside attack. The options that offer shots within 15 feet of the basket become the desired ones. No outside options or long shots can be taken during this play to protect a lead. Much time must be spent in practicing this part of the game. The type of shot taken at this time must be a 75 to 80 percent possibility and not the 36 to 40 per cent type which can be taken earlier in the game with less risk.

You Must Be Able to Control the Ball

The control game is also a very important phase of any offensive attack. The control situation exists when a team ahead in the score needs to control possession. Because of control play the other team must gamble, and your team may score the layup or be fouled by the opponents. The point of the game when your team goes into this style of attack is debated yearly by the second guesser's club. Some experts contend you should have a two-point lead for each minute remaining. The time of this change in attack will vary before you "let the air out of the ball." The control pattern must depend on things taken into consideration by the coach. These would be scouting reports of the opponent and the ability of his team to meet the possibilities.

Some coaches contend a team can control the ball with the same attack they have used during the earlier part of the game. It is the contention of other coaches that some changes be made in the attack. The center of the play area can be opened by moving the post man out and having him operate in a five-man weave. During this attack a premium must be placed on good passing, good screening, and change up cutting for the basket. The only shot attempted at this time should be the cinch shot, or the layup— and that is often missed. The team trailing in the score must gamble to gain possession of the ball or it cannot hope to win. With the pressure on the team behind in the score, mistakes might be more plentiful on its part, thus opening the way to score.

Some control games are taken over by a clever dribbler. The other team must double team or foul this player to stop his effectiveness. During this dribble control by one team member, the other four members hug the side line, to keep their men out and provide space for the dribbler.

The Defense Must Be Spread for Control Purposes

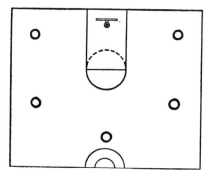 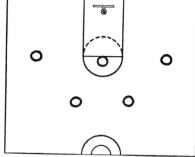

Fig. 32. Open center control game attack.

Fig. 33. High post control game attack.

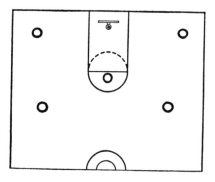

Fig. 34. Side interchange control game attack.

Keeping the defense spread and allowing room for movement will create openings. Avoid double team situations. Stay away from the corners and the side and end lines. Maintain a reasonable distance from the mid-court line to prevent the defense from forcing you over the ten second line. Crowding the line may cause a violation and subsequent loss of the ball.

A careful pass and a drive toward the basket will keep the defense balanced. Occasionally on an over-play, trying for an interception, the defense may set up a change of direction. Such a maneuver will allow a change up and cut toward the basket for a pass and scoring attempt. When there is any doubt about the chances of making the layup, the shot should not be attempted. The player must continue out and start the play again. Retaining possession of the ball is the desired objective until there is a chance for an easy basket.

Despite hours of practice spent on this phase of the game, there is always the player who will take the shot he shouldn't, and risk loss of possession. This characteristic on the part of the players who forget momentarily in their desire to win may cause you to "lose some religion." Such unpredictability in the actions of the players is one of the factors contributing to unpredictability in scores, and is often responsible for your losing the close ones. As coach, you would do well to drill into your player that unless a shot looks certain he should not take it. Repetition of this principle will educate and discipline your team more firmly in the do's and don'ts of the ball control action of the game.

ZONE ATTACK WITH VARIATIONS

When the rules committee widened the free throw lane, some critics of the game and of the rules committee contended the zone defense would be more widely employed. Even though popular opinion believed this to be unlikely, it did occur. Many teams were caught unprepared to combat the zone defense and lost games through the surprise element. If a team is prepared to meet a zone, it should be able to get good shots by excellent passing and moving the ball. If an attack is to be successful, your percentage of shots made must be good against any type of defense. When the zone defense masses men and concentrates on the ball, the offense must penetrate the zone as well as shoot over it. The attempt to score inside must be made against the zone at least one third of the time. Failure to get the inside shot will favor the zone and lessen your chance to penetrate the defense.

Let's look at the purposes of the zone defense:

1. To curb the driving and screening game.
2. To increase rebound strength.
3. To create an opportunity for fast break.
4. To force the long shot.
5. To keep key men from fouling out.
6. To develop ball hawks.
7. To take advantage of small floors.

What are the simplest ways to beat a zone?

1. Good ball handling.
2. Strong outside shooting.

What Is the Best Attack for the Zone?

Most zone defenses cannot be attacked with the same method used against a man-for-man defense. Since the zone has become more popular, changes have been introduced into the offensive attack with better results. Some teams are using an attack which with little variation can be used against both types of defense. The tandem offense is one.

In attacking a zone, keep the following objectives in mind:

1. Move the ball well inside and out.
2. Aim at overloading and employ cutters through the defense.
3. Place men in open spots to prompt a change to man-for-man tactics.
4. The best way to beat the zone defense is to bring the ball quickly down the floor and attack the zone before it can be set up strongly.

Types of Zone Defense

Many zones are used today to take advantage of certain personnel and to save time in teaching. The placing of the men will generally describe the type of zone. These are illustrated in Figures 35-42.

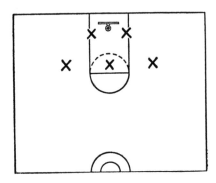

Fig. 35.   3-2 zone.

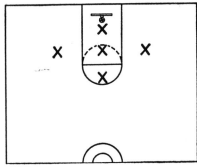

Fig. 36.   2-3 zone.

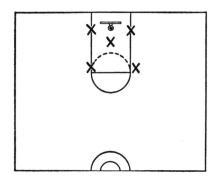

Fig. 37.   2-1-2 zone.

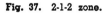

Fig. 38.   1-3-1 zone.

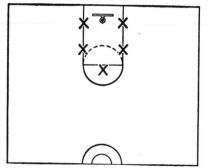

Fig. 39. 1-2-2 zone.

Fig. 40. 2-2-1 zone.

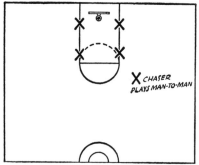

Fig. 41. Box and chaser.

Fig. 42. Combination front line man-to-man and back line zone principles and vice versa.

Attacking the 3-2 Zone

Players in the offensive attack must be placed according to the open spots in the zone. There are two variations of attack against the 3-2 zone. These attacks are the 2-1-2 attack and the 1-3-1 attack. The center man in each of these attacks may be moved

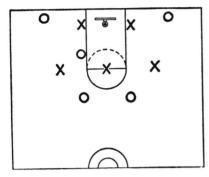 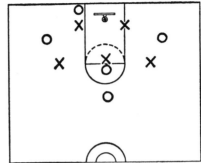

Fig. 43. Placement of men in 2-1-2 attack.   **Fig. 44.** Placement of men in 1-3-1 attack.

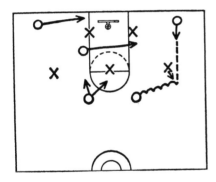 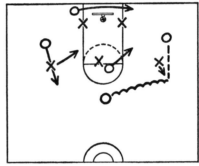

Fig. 45. 2-1-2 attack overload
principle either side.

Fig. 46. 1-3-1 attack overload principle
either side.

slightly to force the defense to protect the middle at all costs. In the 2-1-2 attack, either of the attacking front men can go to the side to pull the defensive wing man out with him. As the pass is made from the front man to the corner man, the inside back defensive man must move out to cover him. At this point the center man playing in front of the free throw line, moves to the side of the ball. This move forces the zone to drop back to fill the middle.

The opposite base line man on the offense as well as the opposite front man can move to the openings caused by the defensive shift.

In the 1-3-1 attack, the baseline man moves as a floater to the side of the ball. He must not go too far toward the corner. This maneuver would make the shot attempt too long. The high post man playing at the free throw line also moves to the side of the ball. Thus an overload situation is created and a double triangle is formed with the four men on the side of the ball. The opposite wing man will need to come out toward the mid-court line to protect position for defensive possibilities. If the wing man shoots, he should never follow his own shot as the overload favors his side. The congestion will not allow the wing man shooting to get on the boards effectively. The front man who is the key feeder of the attack should be mobile, moving to either side of the defense for good angle passing opportunities. The floater along the baseline and the high post man should possess good rebounding and close shooting abilities. The two wing men should be fast and be able to shoot from outside. The front man in the attack must be smart, able to diagnose movements of the defense, and be the best shooter and passer on the squad.

Attacking the 2-3 and the 2-1-2 Zone

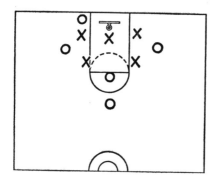

Fig. 47. Placement of men attacking a 2-3 zone.

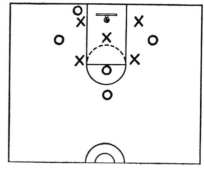

Fig. 48. Placement of men attacking a 2-1-2 zone.

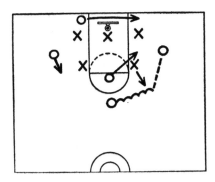

Fig. 49. 2-3 zone attack overload principle either side.

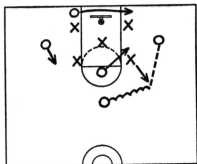

Fig. 50. 2-1-2 zone attack overload principle either side.

The 2-3 and the 2-1-2 zones are much alike due to the placing of the men in the defense. In the 2-3 zone the middle man plays closer to the basket. He may maneuver at times to also set up the 2-1-2 zone.

The 1-3-1 attack is generally conceded the best attack against these two zones. By placing these men in this attack the overload can be set up easily by moving the ball. At the same time the men move also to the ball side. The floater along the baseline moves to the side of the ball, attempting to get the 10-foot shot. The high post man also moves with the ball to create a double triangle with the wing man and the feeder. As in other 1-3-1 attacks the opposite wing man must move toward mid-court to protect with the feeder. Shots are easily obtained when the wing man passes to the floater or the post man for shooting opportunities. The floater, the post man, and the opposite wing man make up the rebounding triangle. In the 1-3-1 attack the front feeder should never penetrate beyond the free throw line unless he is used as a cutter through.

Attacking the 1-3-1 Zone

To defend against the high-scoring pivot-man, the 1-3-1 zone was introduced to place defensive men in front and in back of the

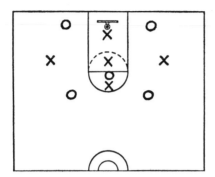

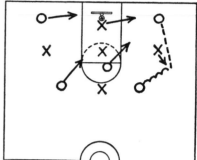

Fig. 51. Placement of men attacking 1-3-1 zone.

Fig 52. Attacking 1-3-1 zone; overload principle either side.

big post man. With the men placed in these two positions defensively, good double teaming advantages were established. The main objective of this zone defense was to keep the ball from getting to the big post man. When several teams began to use the 1-3-1 zone attack, coaches countered the strategy by using the 1-3-1 zone. Where offensive play was determined by moving the ball only against the zone this defensive play resulted in playing man-to-man tactics. With no screening or cutting by the offense, the defense had a terrific advantage. A realignment of the offensive men was then necessary to force the defense to cover new areas.

The 2-1-2 attack against the 1-3-1 zone forces pressure on the deep defensive man. If the front attacker maneuvers to get the pass in to one of the baseline men, the wing defensive man is forced to come out to play him. As the pass is made to the corner man on the baseline, the deep defensive man must adjust to cover this man. The defense is then forced to drop front men back, opening the center area. In case the front line does not drop back, the opposite corner baseline man is open as he moves toward the ball. When the front line drops back, the center or the opposite front man move into open areas for the pass and the shot. Rebounding becomes the responsibility of the two inside baseline men and the high post man. Personnel must be placed wisely to meet the demands of the offensive attack and to capitalize on individual offensive abilities.

Attacking the 1-2-2 Zone

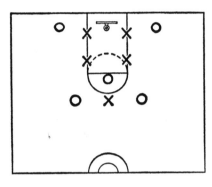

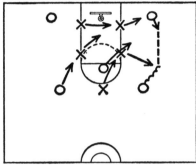

Fig. 53. Placement of men attacking 1-2-2 zone.

Fig. 54. Attacking 1-2-2 zone; overload principle either side.

The 1-2-2 zone is sometimes referred to as the "jug type" zone. This term indicates that men are placed on the ball so that the formation resembles a gallon jug. One man in this zone is always playing the ball while the other four form the shoulders and base of the jug defense. The inside shot will be difficult; the good shot exists in the 15-foot area.

It is imperative that the side front man of the offense dribble to the side to pull the corner defensive man out. When the corner man moves out to cover, the high post man moves to the opened area. The pass can go to either the corner man or the center. This pass will force the outside base man to be between two offensive men. The opposite front offensive player can key on the defensive man nearest him and move to the openings created when the defense adjusts. The rebounding assignment goes to the two baseline men and the center. Again the placing of players is important and their abilities must be utiliized to meet this zone defense successfully.

Attacking the 2-2-1 Zone

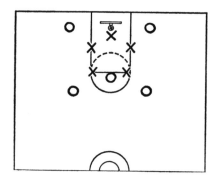

Fig. 55. Placement of men attacking 2-2-1 zone.

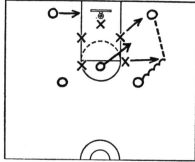

Fig. 56. Attacking 2-2-1 zone; overload principle either side.

The 2-2-1 zone is exactly the opposite of the 1-2-2 zone. The attack can be effected by placing two men along the base-line to put pressure on the one deep defensive man. The defense is forced to compensate to match this situation. When the front man dribbles to the side, the defense must move out to play him. This movement creates an opening for the center to get good position for a shot. The single defensive man in front of the basket cannot cover the distance between the baseline men. The rear defensive wing man must give his teammate help. This creates an offensive advantage of 2 on 1. The front opposite offensive player keys on the defensive man nearest him and adjusts to take the open area. The rebounding is strong with the three inside men assuming the assignment.

Attacking the Box and Chaser

The box and chaser combination defense can be very confusing if a team is not prepared to meet it. This defense features four

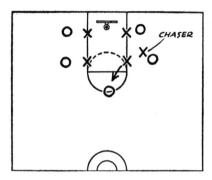

Fig. 57. Placement of men in box and chaser defense.

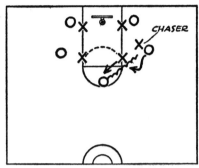

Fig. 58. Attacking box and chaser with screen.

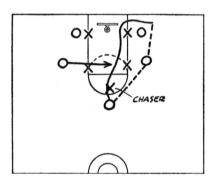

Fig. 59. Attacking box and chaser with cutter through.

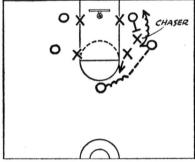

Fig. 60. Attacking box and chaser with blind screen.

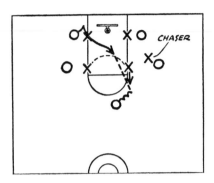

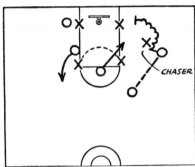

Fig. 61. Attacking box and chaser   Fig. 62. Attacking box and chaser
with base line man in free throw area.   with 1-on-1 situation.

men playing zone principles and one man playing a strict man-to-man defense. In most cases the best offensive player is defensed man-to-man over the half court area or inside the usual defensive zone. Screening tactics can be used to allow the offensive man to shoot over a screen. If a screen and drive technique is employed, the defensive men playing the box zone will pick the player up in their respective areas.

In some instances one-on-one matching may be effective if the offensive man can work the side area and outmaneuver his opponent. The shot will have to be taken outside the free throw area, however. You can attack this defense by employing a cutter through to overload the baseline.

The offense must set its pattern to spread the defense as much as possible. Placing men from 3 to 6 feet outside the free throw area will force the box to play you. The center offensive man can dribble to either side and set a screen for the shooter. The baseline man can also move out to place a blind screen on the chaser. When the cutter goes through, the baseline man can screen and the cutter may have a good 10 foot shot. The opposite wing man can move to the free throw line for a good shot. Good rebounding position will also result with this move.

Occasionally the baseline man can break into the free throw lane to get a good shot when the defense remains in the zone. In any event, the chaser must be taken outside to get good screening and maneuvering opportunities. If the chaser is taken inside, the defense becomes more massed and the shot opportunities are limited and more difficult. The box and chaser defense is being used more each year. With a slight change of attack, the offense can meet it much as it would attack the regular zone. This eliminates the necessity of confusing the players with a new attack. With this defense being similar to the 1-2-2 jug defense, the attack can be made effective with a few options to take care of the chaser.

Combination Zone Attack

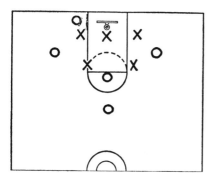

Fig. 63. Placement of men in combination zone attack.

Fig. 64. Combination zone attack with screens and cutters.

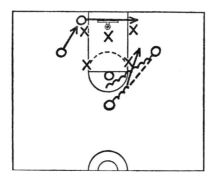

Fig. 65. Combination zone attack with screens and cutters.

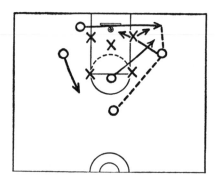

Fig. 66. Combination zone attack with screens and cutters.

The combination zone may feature a front line man-to-man principle with the rear line playing zone. Or this procedure may be reversed. You must move with cutters to take care of the problems. To stand and pass the ball would create no openings, as the defense will play you man-to-man all the way.

Sometimes this type of defense will attempt to confuse you by changing tactics. One time the defense may be in a zone; next time down the floor the defense may be in a man-to-man. Your team will only be confused if it tries to counter this changing strategy by meeting each defense accordingly. You should always have a set play which will determine the defense. Sending one man through the defense and back to the front line will help you determine the defense. If the defensive unit follows him all the way, the defense can be playing man-to-man. If the front line of the defense checks him to the rear line, zone principles are being employed. When there is a question regarding the defense employed, this should be the offensive measure to detect the defense.

Tandem Offensive Attack

The tandem post attack with screens and cutters will present situations to trouble changing defenses. Many teams use this offensive attack to meet both situations. If there are changing tactics by the defense, your team can force the defense to play man-to-man by using the high-low post attack. If the defense goes man-to-man, the screening and driving options are very effective.

In this offensive attack, the baseline floater should go to the side of the ball. If the floater is on the side of the pass, he can maneuver out to take his man with him. This attack against the zone uses overload principles. Patterns employing screens will worry the man-to-man defense. Many coaches contend the tandem offense to be the answer in adjusting to any type defense more readily. As a result, this offensive attack may be used exclusively.

Attacking the Press and Semi-Press Defense

The press and semi-press defense, like the zone, can be very bewildering to your team if you haven't prepared the team to meet it. The element of surprise and unpreparedness makes these two variations of defense worth while. The press and semi-press is not too difficult to attack. When the defense covers more of an area of the playing floor, openings should be better. It stands to reason that the defense cannot spread and restrict movement. When the defense elects to play you tight on a full court, screens and change-ups can be worked more effectively.

You will have to consider these possibilities:

1. Congesting the offense for screens.
2. Spreading the defense for maneuverability.
3. Recognizing the 10-second rule to get the ball across.

After you have moved the ball over the mid-court line, the same attack you ordinarily use against man-to-man principles will work. This is true especially if the opponents continue to play you tight. In addition to the regular attack being more effective, such techniques as give and go, change of direction, blind screens, and cutaways will be effective. These movements will force the press defense into a more conservative defense. Good dribbling can also be used to get the ball into the attacking area.

There Is a Zone Press, Too

Some teams will use a form of zone press with the press and semi-press. Your team must be able to recognize the zone press immediately. The full court press succeeds because of double team situations, interceptions, and confusion of the offense. The semi-press attempts to accomplish some of these objectives. The half court or semi-press will meet your attack at mid-court. The defense will try to force you into making errors. If they cannot force your team to make mistakes, they hope to make you set your attack far enough from the basket to reduce the screening strength inside. The side men and the post men are contested vigorously to keep the ball away from them.

The zone press is used with the other two press defenses. The method of attacking the press and semi-press fits in well with the zone press principle. Most teams attack the press and semi-press with dribbling or cross screening. This method of attack will play directly into the hands of the zone press team. Consequently, your strategy of play will have to be changed when the zone press is recognized. Sometimes it becomes difficult to recognize these variations. Before a team can adjust to the situation, the zone press may hurt it.

The Full Court Press

As mentioned previously, there are two methods used to attack the full court press. There is the congested attack and the spread attack. Your team will operate better and have more chance to succeed if it forces the defense to spread. When your team recognizes the full court press, the big men should go down the floor. The smaller men can then operate without interference. The back court men must be thoroughly trained to meet the situation. Sometimes the big man attempts to get into the act and trouble is the result.

In case your little men get into trouble, the other men should be in position to help quickly. Often a team will relax when the defense allows it to penetrate the scoring area without a contest. As a result, the front court men get in a habit of not looking back to see developments. When the opponents put a full court press on, the back court men may be in trouble. If the men down court are not aware of this possibility, the back court men may have trouble. The front court men should always be aware of this possibility and

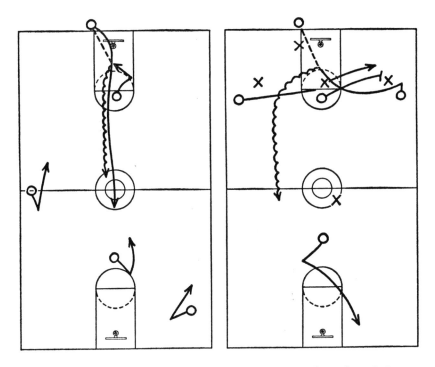

Fig. 67. Spread attack against press. **Fig. 68.** Congested attack against press.

be ready to help. They should frequently look back down the floor; it will help them to recover in time, if help is needed.

You should drill your back court men every day in perfecting this attack. While the inside men are working on rebounding, the back court men can drill on getting the ball down the floor. On an out-of-bounds situation, both men must be able to maneuver in angles to receive the pass. Sometimes the defense will drop off the man out of bounds and double team the intended receiver. This procedure will place a defensive man in front of and in back of the possible receiver. If the receiver of the pass in doesn't know how to maneuver in angles and with sharp changes of direction, he will never be free to receive the pass.

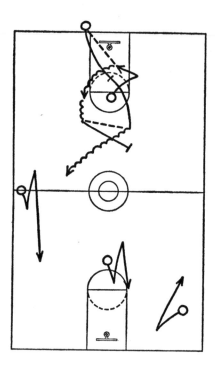

Fig.69. Attacking a press by cross-screening.

The pass receiver must never run in circles. He must also stay away from the sidelines. When the press is put on at other times with the ball inbounds, the offensive man should be able to out-maneuver his defensive man. It is always a good rule to avoid long lob passes that can be covered easily while the ball is in flight. Avoiding cross-court passes which can be easily intercepted is also good strategy.

Spread the Defense Out

When two offensive men are given the assignment to get the pass in bounds, you can work various two-man plays to move the ball down court. When using the spread attack, place your front line men down court. One man should be at mid-court near the side-line. The center can place himself at the head of the offensive free throw circle. The third man needs to go to the distant offensive corner. The mid-court man and the post man are then in good position to help if needed.

After the pass is made inbounds, the passer can form interference for his teammate to dribble. When the defense drifts, the dribbler will be able to advance the ball without interference. If the defense attempts to double team the dribbler, the man in front can break away for a return pass. This situation may force a switch and result in the offense having an advantage by outnumbering the defense. Often the side man or the center can move toward the ball to blind screen the defense. When this happens and the defense is forced to switch, a cutaway toward the basket is effective. After the ball is taken across the center line, your ordinary plan of attack will be effective. If the defense still presses tight past the center line, your screens should be very effective. When the opponents switch or double team, your opportunity to overmatch increases, and the basket attempts should be easier to obtain.

You Can Cross Screen, Too

The players assigned the responsibility of bringing the ball down court may cross screen or cut-away if the opponents press. With a variation of trailer tactics with cross screening, the opposition will be unable to play the percentages. You can keep them from forcing you to play their style. When the same method of advancing the ball is used on a stereotyped basis, the defense is able to prepare to meet the mechanical operation. You must always keep the opponent off balance by change-ups in maneuvering. When these tactics are varied, the opponents will have to vary their defensive tactics. Successful basketball is achieved when you can out-maneuver and outsmart your opposition.

The Semi-Press Attack

The semi-press method of defensive play will usually allow your team to advance to mid-court without contest. At the 10-second

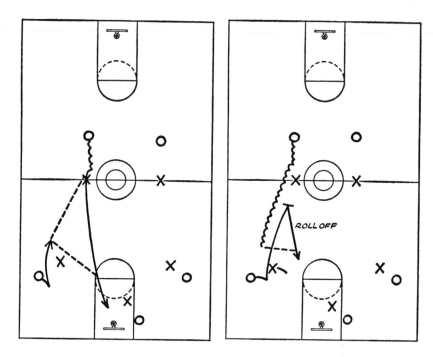

Fig. 70. Attacking a semi-press with a give-and-go.

Fig. 71. Attacking a semi-press with a blind screen.

line, however, the defense will tighten and make it tough to get inside. When the front line men contest at mid-court, the back court defense will overplay and contest any passes in. Most of the maneuvers used by the offense against the full court press can be used successfully against the semi-press. The following maneuvers will pay off:

1. Change of direction.
2. Give and go.
3. Roll-off screens.
4. Cut away from screens.
5. Blind screen the defense.

By using these maneuvers, your attack will force the defense to the head of the free throw circle where you can operate efficiently with your regular attack. Blind screening will worry the pressing defensive man. When you can create worry in the minds of the defense, you decrease their efficiency as individuals.

Your team must keep calm and poised against any press. When panic strikes a team, it is more apt to make mistakes. The semi-press defense, if successful, will sometimes force your offense to start farther from the basket. At this stage, open maneuvers will be more successful than a strict pattern attack.

The Zone Press Attack

The zone press attack is executed with two or three men playing zone tactics in the near court. The object of this defense is to force the dribbler into a double team situation. Bad passes or tie-ups for jump balls will result. Stealing the ball is often the result. It is a waste of time to advance the ball with a dribble against a zone press. This offensive strategy will backfire and allow your team's play to favor the defense.

When the zone press is used against you, your team must be ready to recognize it and attack it. The ball must be passed over the front line zone. If the pass is not made quickly over the zone, congestion of men will result. Players down floor must come back to meet the ball as it is passed. The short pass is more effective in this attack than the long or lob pass. Double team situations will be more easily avoided and the defense can be made to spread more.

In case you meet a three-man zone with a tandem, the quick pass over will give you an advantage. This advantage will be a three-on-two set-up. The play must be hurried at this stage to capitalize on the advantage before the defense recovers. The zone press is difficult to recognize when it is used with variations of other pressing defenses. Much drill is needed to prepare a team for the possibilities of these defenses. When your team is not prepared to meet these defenses with confidence, poise and the proper attack, the evening could be a long one.

Attacking the Shifting Man-To-Man Defense

It is easily understood that having a separate attack for each variation of defense could result in confusion. In most cases slight

Fig. 72. Roll-off against switch.   **Fig. 73.** Cut-away against switch.

optional maneuvers will compensate for and take advantage of the defensive action. The shifting man-to-man defense will curtail somewhat the driving game. It will also affect your screening game if adjustments aren't made. With a slight change of maneuver on the part of the offense, the driving and screening game will still be effective against the shifts. Two maneuvers make this possible: the roll-off and the cut-away. The offensive man can gain a favorable position in both.

To make the roll-off effective, the screener must approach the opponent in an attempt to set an ordinary screen. When his teammate comes off the screen forcing a switch, the screener pivots off the inside foot. As the pivot is made the defense is blocked momentarily and the screener breaks for the basket. This gives him a step advantage to receive a pass from his teammate. The offensive man coming off the screen must gain distance to the side to force the switching man with him. The angle pass is better executed to the cutter as the defense is forced out. If the man off the screen stops too soon, the pass has to be made to the blind side of the cutter. Three men are in a line also when the defense is allowed to stop. To pass over three men is dangerous and difficult. When the defense buttonhooks well on this maneuver, the screener may have to penetrate farther and set the screen more to the rear of the defensive man.

When using the cut-away technique, the screener attempts to get position by getting his outside foot behind the defensive man's inside foot. When this position is obtained, the screener can turn to the inside and take a lead step toward the basket. The pass can be made as the screener breaks away from the defense. His teammate must make the defensive man switch toward the direction of the sideline to make the good angle pass in. Deeper screens must also be set in this maneuver. The pass must be made the instant the cut-away man is free. Any delay on the part of the screener or passer may allow the defense to recover. Switching tactics have to be effected on definite cross or straight screens. Give-and-go tactics may be used with good results when the opposition attempts to switch on screens.

A Trailer Will Be Successful Also

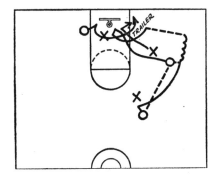
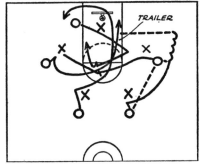

Fig. 74. Trailer play off switch.   **Fig. 75.** Trailer play off double screen.

In addition to the roll-off and cut-away, a trailer coming back off the switch will open for a pass and shot because of position. This maneuver must be well timed, and consequently needs much practice to perfect. On every screening situation on the ball, the handoff man must turn in the direction of the handoff. When a player turns this way he can see the switch occur quicker and diagnose the play better. He can also gain position by blocking off the defensive man with his back. If a turn is made opposite the handoff, he cannot see the switch soon enough and the defense can recover.

The trailer technique is more successful when the switching tactics are employed off the ball. When the defense switches to pick the man off the screen, he stops and sets a screen for the man who screened initially. As the trailer stops he has position on the switch and comes back to get the pass and a good shot over the screen set by the teammate he was attempting to help. Sometimes a switching defense is mistaken for a zone. When in doubt you may send a player through the defense to determine defensive play.

Attacking the Sagging Defense

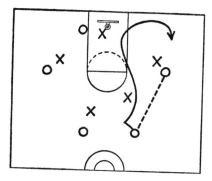

Fig. 76. Send man through defense.

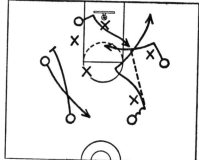

Fig. 77. Exchange off ball.

Basketball teams will use the sagging defense against a team of poor shooters. The defenders will sag back to invite the long shot. In some cases teams will have single defensive men drop back and let a poor shooter go. This maneuver will allow the team to double up on effective shooters to reduce their scoring efficiency. When the defense does this to your team, the weak shooter must move inside the defense. When he is inside the defense, his shooting threat increases and forces the defense to cover him. The chance to double team will also be minimized with this attack.

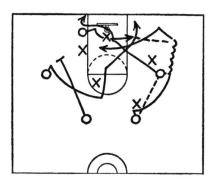

Fig. 78. Exchange off ball with delayed
screen.

Sagging defenses will also be used against a good inside shooter. Many times the inside man is the post man. It is almost impossible to stop good hook shooters if they get the ball. In contesting the pass in to a post man, the defense must overplay his side. If the side is played or the defense plays in front of the post man, the defensive man can be blocked off with a pivot to receive the pass. The majority of sagging defenses on a post man will collapse the men off the side of the ball. When these men collapse, the offensive men must learn to play without the ball. This is always a must but more so against the sagging defense. When the offensive men change position off the ball, defensive men will be occupied enough to reduce the double team.

When the offense changes position off the ball, the defense must be aware of the movement. During this awareness, a delayed screener can be used successfully to bring a man down the middle. This option will force the opponent to come out on the exchange if he avoids the screen. When pressure like this is placed on men off the ball, there will be less chance to congest the middle area and double up on your post man. When teams collapse or sag on the side of the ball, distance is too big a factor. The ball can be passed faster than the man can move and shots are easy to get. The sagging defense is a combination type with three men on the ball playing man-for-man, and the two men off the ball playing a zone. Exchanging men will force the men playing zone to cover with a tighter defense.

Special Situations

There are many special patterns in basketball that must be treated with the care and details of other situations. Some teams devote many hours to perfecting these possibilities. Other teams will free-lance and take what comes. Your team will have more success in these special cases if its play is organized with a definite purpose. The time spent in practicing and perfecting movements off these opportunities will be profitable. If a score is not attained, possession of the ball will be guaranteed to carry on your attack.

Jump Balls

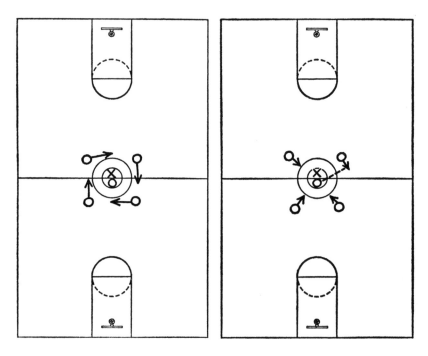

Fig. 79. Clockwise rotation offensive formation.   Fig. 80. Decoy offensive formation.

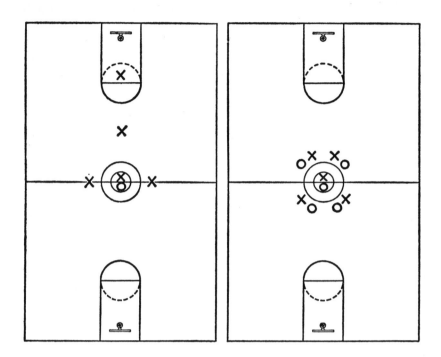

Fig. 81. Defensive formation.   **Fig. 82.** Defensive formation.

Every time there is a jump ball, there is a chance for possession by either team. When your team can gain possession the greater number of times, your chances for scoring will increase. As the ball is tossed for the jump, your team is placed in an offensive or defensive position. This is determined by the size and jumping ability of the two players concerned with the tip. If you can control the tip, your team will maneuver to gain possession. If you cannot control the jump, you must take every precaution to keep the other team from scoring. At the same time you must attempt to gain possession by outmaneuvering or outsmarting your opponents.

Some teams will use a regular pattern for jump balls at the start of the game and at the beginning of the second half. This pattern or definite play will use screening options to shake men loose. Other teams will free lance and attempt to decoy and move into tipping areas. When decoying men, the player will purposely draw the defense out of the area where he can screen him and move into a tipping zone designated with signals. Sometimes the play is so simple in execution it works. The opponents think you are too smart to work with simplicity. It is necessary, regardless, to have organization at this time. Practice and organization will adequately prepare your team to operate with confidence in these situations.

Rotation of men from a box formation will help to gain control of the tipped ball. By pre-arranged signal the four men may move clockwise or counter-clockwise into specific areas. The ball is tipped to a predetermined point and a man is assigned to come up with the ball. Moving men out from the circle approximately six to eight feet will draw the opponent out with you. When the ball is tipped, you can move the man in to gain better position to get possession. Every jump ball situation must be organized and not left to chance if you are to get the tip by either jumper.

Statistics on all jump balls during games and scrimmages are very worthwhile. They not only give you information on possession but also on jumping abilities. All of your players should be taught to jump higher and more effectively. Teaching techniques of facing the opponent properly with arm and shoulder swing up is important. The leg action should be coordinated with other parts of the body to reach greater height on jumps. When your players have been taught to jump, your smaller men may outjump a larger opponent and get possession for your team at a crucial time in the game. Your practice schedule should include jumping and tipping practice. You should also take your squad through the jump ball opportunities at all three circles to acquaint them with the best strategy to employ when the same situation occurs in a game.

Out-of-Bounds Situations

During a game many out-of-bounds situations will occur in front and back court. In the front court situations you must be prepared to maneuver to get the ball in bounds safely. A good-percentage shot should be the aim of such a play. If the good shot is not ob-

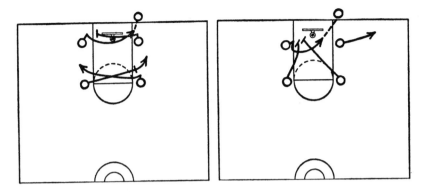

Fig. 83. Out-of-bounds on end line.   Fig. 84. Out-of-bounds on end line.

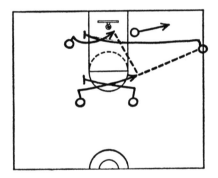

Fig. 85. Out-of-bounds on side line.

tained, organization of the situation will at least assure possession and a continuation of the attack. Time spent in preparation for the out-of-bounds situations will be profitable both ways—to attempt a score and to assure possession of the ball. Many scores can result from organized offensive play on an out of bounds opportunity.

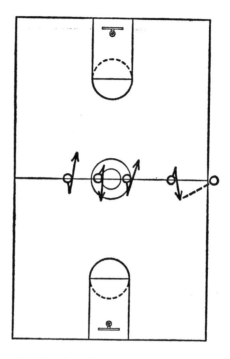

Fig. 86.   Out-of-bounds at mid-court line.

If your team can score one or two baskets a game off your front court out-of-bounds play, the time and effort spent in practice is well compensated. If you do not get your shot or score, you can still spread the defense and allow good offensive balance to get the ball in. In back court play your team must know a few tricks to get the ball in play from out of bounds against a good pressing defense.

Areas for Out-of-Bounds Action in Front Court

Three areas will be involved in out-of-bounds play in front court. These areas are the end line, the side line and mid-court. Your team must have organization to get the ball in play in each area. The end and side line possibilities exist in out-of-bounds play when violations by the other team occur. Also when the ball is caused to be out of play by your opponents. The mid-court possibility is present after a technical foul or by other means previously mentioned.

In past years, teams were allowed by the rules to waive free throws and take possession of the ball at mid-court. Out-of-bounds plays during the contest, and especially toward the end of the game, were plentiful and productive. Since the rule was changed, however, the opportunities at mid-court have been lessened and little time is now spent in perfecting plays for the mid-court situation. As a coach, however, you must prepare your team for this situation. When the team knows what to do, the opponents are less apt to win a close game if there is a planned play to get the ball in bounds.

There are many plays that may be devised and used with success, depending on your personnel. Considerable planning and thought must precede the proper use of players' proficiency for better results. For example, it would be unwise to have your smallest player attempt to get the ball in on certain occasions in front court.

Free Throw Situations

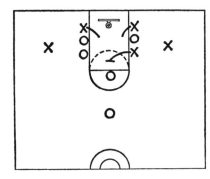
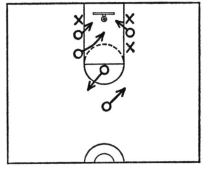

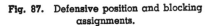

Fig. 87. Defensive position and blocking assignments.

Fig. 88. Offensive maneuver.

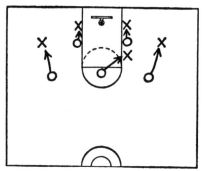

Fig. 89. Press off free throw.

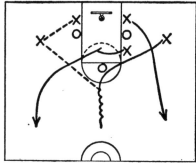

Fig. 90. Fast break off free throw.

With the average number of free throws increasing during the last five years, this phase of the game has become more important. Not only the free throw line, but also the sides of the free throw area are important. When the rules allowed defensive men to take position in both the inside zones, strategy along the lane changed. The angle of approach in attempting to get the ball is much different than previously. The inside men will force their action away from the basket with a step to block out the opponent. The offensive men next to the inside lanes will try to step toward the basket to gain position. The other positions along the lane retain equal importance to achieve definite assignments. The defense will be working to get the missed shot and start their attack. The offense will be attempting to keep possession or tip to score.

As a consequence, all players must be versed on the possibilities in playing the free throw. Knowing what to do at the proper time is sometimes the difference in winning the closely contested games. Your team should be taught how to play these situations and checked during scrimmages and drills to help eliminate the mistakes that exist in competition with key opponents.

Many teams made better use of the pressing defense on a free throw situation when the defense was given both inside areas. The defensive possibilities were matched better and quicker pickups were made when equal matching of men was present. Your team must know how to handle this possibility. Some teams attempt fast break attacks off the made or missed free throw. You may do the same thing. Scoring a quick and easy basket off these possibilities will help to increase the score with a minimum of effort. The tendency to do this at any time will keep the defense out and increase the chances for your team.

In conclusion, it is common knowledge that you cannot develop a separate offensive attack to meet each variation of defensive play. Any basic man-to-man offense, whether, for example, it be single post, double post, or weave combination, can include slight offensive maneuvers to adjust to defensive strategy. You should develop a uniform attack to meet all types of zone defense. The 1-3-1 attack is considered the best for this need. You can use a 1-3-1 zone attack with an overloading principle, send cutters through, or plan a revolving attack to fit your personnel.

The various possibilities have been presented to stimulate thinking and to offer variations you might adapt to your squad. Simplicity of attack will still complement success in coaching. Sufficient plays and options must be used, however, to make your attack effective. Insufficient play patterns will permit the defense to stymie your attack. You will need as a minimum offense a fast break, a set attack, a zone offense, an attack for a press, a control game and development of special situations. Anything perfected beyond this will be a tribute to your ability and will indicate good planning and good organization.

• 2 •

How to Select the Best Offensive Attack

Which Offensive Plan Is Best?

Three factors must be present if your basketball offensive system is to be successful.

1. It must be sound.
2. It must fit your team.
3. You, as coach, must know the system thoroughly and teach it effectively.

These three requirements are so interrelated, each one dependent on the other, that one without the others will result in only average performance. Carefully weigh your team's size, speed, passing and shooting skills, and other individual and team abilities in setting up the best possible offensive system. Your faith in the system and a knowledge of it will be instrumental in its successful operation. Further, this belief in your attack and its possibilities must be imparted to your players, otherwise they will not have the confidence necessary to develop their full potential.

Which plan of attack is best for the team lacking height? For the team with exceptional speed? With several distance-shot aces?

54

Or a team lacking in depth? Although these considerations are all important, you should never change your style of play simply for the sake of change. More often than not, a sudden change means failure.

Don't Change Horses in Mid-Stream

Sometimes you encounter a system which looks seemingly better and easier to teach than your present one. Take heart. Most likely your team is having an off-night and your opponent looks exceptionally good. Remember your system is the one you know best and you may have difficulty teaching another type of play without adequate advance preparation.

If you contemplate a change, devote time to intensive investigation, study the new system before adopting it. Adjusting your system to your squad's abilities may require several seasons. Actually, the process of making a gradual change has its advantage: variations in attack will require more attention by opponents in combating your variations. Thus they must concentrate on defense.

New ideas and innovations initiated by other coaches can be worked into your system with good results. Remember that you are never too smart to learn from your opponents, your players, and your colleagues in the profession. In short, if you can't beat them, join them.

Fundamental Execution Is Important

Regardless of the offensive system selected, it will not operate well unless the various skills and techniques are mastered. The system must also be basically sound. Books are full of plays and patterns, but none will be successful unless a team is able to pass, shoot, dribble, and maneuver well enough to make the system work. Stress small details of execution. Be a "stickler" and insist on proper execution of plays and reactions to meet the defensive adjustments of the opposition. This is achieved only after much practice and repetition of the pattern and its operation. In the insistence of proper execution while teaching routine, you must certainly display patience.

Basketball is a game of habits. Drill helps to make necessary movements become automatic through repetition. Many times little maneuvers which seem unimportant can mean the difference between success and failure of a play. Simplicity of attack must be stressed to your players and the number of plays in your repertoire kept to a minimum. You cannot burden young players with too many details or none are mastered. Many young coaches fail in the profession because they overburden their players. Due to this "over coaching," the players have more than they can learn and become confused to the point where nothing is done well. A few plays, with variations of options to meet defensive changes, will meet most needs. These few plays, however, must be well executed and will be more successful than many plays taught poorly and worked ineffectively. Simplicity in attack is basic in most sports regardless of the level of competition.

Single-Post System and Plays

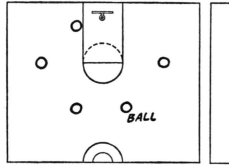 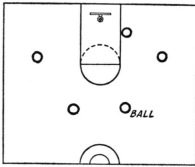

Fig. 91. Single post system with post man opposite the ball.   **Fig. 92.** Single post system with post man on the ball.

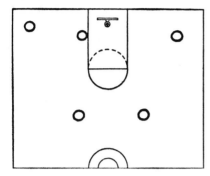

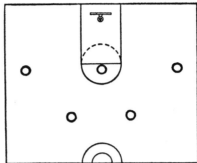

Fig. 93. Single post system with side men further inside.

Fig. 94. Single post system with high post position.

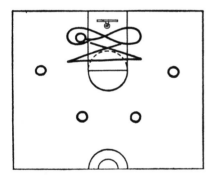

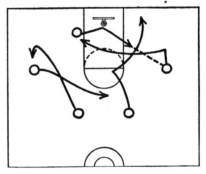

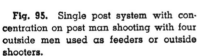

Fig. 95. Single post system with concentration on post man shooting with four outside men used as feeders or outside shooters.

Fig. 96. Single post attack with cutting and screening techniques in splitting the post. Passer always goes first.

Fig. 97. Post man used as a screener on the ball.

Fig. 98. Post man used as a screener off the ball.

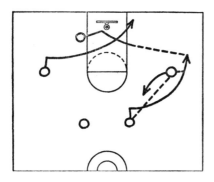

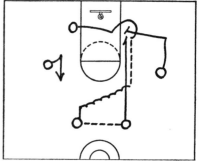

Fig. 99. Post man used as a shooting threat.

Fig. 100. Double screen for post man.

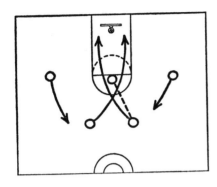 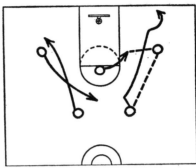

Fig.101. High post maneuver with split.   Fig. 102 High post maneuver for side feed.

The single-post system of offensive play, with its many variations, is probably the oldest and still the most commonly used of all present day attacks. In this system, one player is placed near the free throw area and his abilities are used accordingly.

The tallest man on the squad is usually given this assignment, and if he is near the seven-foot mark and can maneuver well, your single-post play will be more effective. This man may be used strictly as a scoring threat with all plays and action centered around him. He may be used as a combination man in the area which will give better balance to the team attack. Even though the larger man may be placed in this position, many little men have become famous by operating in the post position.

When a large post man is available and he can hook and operate well close in, you can concentrate all of your plays around his abilities.

In most attacks, the post player is placed close to the basket in order to utilize his size and skill. The four supporting players must be able to shoot well from outside in this attack or the defense will collapse to stop the efforts of the post man. In addition to being able to shoot well from outside, the four men must be able to pass in well and handle the ball expertly. In many instances the defense will set up to keep the big post man from getting the ball. Playing in front of the post man or three quarters on the side of the ball will help to stop the feeders from passing to him. Double teaming off the ball is also an effective defense against post men. In this defensive movement, the post man is forced farther from the basket and his play becomes less effective. The close position near the basket adds strength to the rebounding of the team, which is a strong point in post play.

When the post man is used as a combination man, you add to the possibilities of the system. In using the post man's abilities many ways, the attack becomes more versatile. The combination post man is required to shoot, screen, handoff, and rebound. Where these abilities are added with the other four players taking part, the system offers more enjoyment and is more interesting to play. The cutting and screening assault off the post will cause more defensive adjustments and result in more shot opportunities. Splitting the post with one, two, and three cutters is an effective way for all five players to participate. Balance of play and effective driving lanes are also created with the additional movement.

Many little men skilled in faking, maneuvering, and shooting can operate with efficiency in the post position. When a taller, slower man is defensing the little man, the former cannot react quickly enough to defense him properly. Taller men playing defense can be taken away from the board to make equal matching as the taller man is forced out. Unless the small defensive man is familiar with post defense, he will be at a disadvantage. By placing the small man in the post, more defensive adjustments must be made, thereby making the opponents prepare for more possibilities.

The Double-Post System and Plays

When two men are placed close or a medium distance from the basket, it is called the double-post offense. There are two types of double-post play.

1. The narrow type when two men are placed outside the free throw lane where they can operate with screens, shots, and rebounds.

2. The wide type when two men are placed beyond the free throw lane where they force opponents to play one-on-one possibilities or screen for inside play.

The Narrow-Double Post

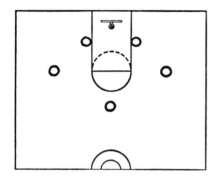

Fig. 103. Narrow double post.

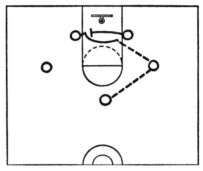

Fig. 104. Cross screening by post men.

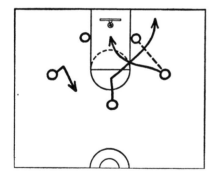

Fig. 105. Splitting post with side feed.

Fig. 106. Three man weave off double post.

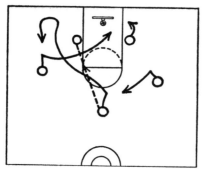

Fig. 107. Splitting the post with front feed.

Fig. 108. Double screen with side feed.

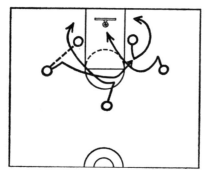

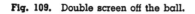

Fig. 109. Double screen off the ball.

Fig. 110. Splitting post with front feed and opposite man coming off split.

When you have two large, slow men on your squad, the narrow double post offense will better fit your personnel. This system can be adapted to close-in shooting as well as good screening possibilities and strong rebounding. In the event two men are placed outside the free throw lane, it is obvious that plays developed by the other three players must take place outside. The play off these two post men will set up the 10 to 15 foot shot. If you have a natural right hander and a natural left hander in the big size, their respective abilities can be utilized for better results. The outside men must be able to drive and shoot well to coordinate this attack.

Front or side feeds by the outside men to the post men can be executed well. Many opportunities for single and double screens exist on the ball and off the ball. Plays and options can be held to a minimum number with good use of all five players in the attack. A three-man weave can be employed with the outside men. Cross screening by the post men will create openings. It was believed by many people that this style of offense would become more popular with the widened free throw lane, but as yet this has not been the case.

The Wide-Double Post

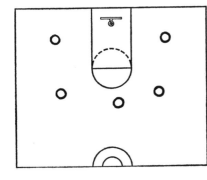

Fig. 111. Wide double post.

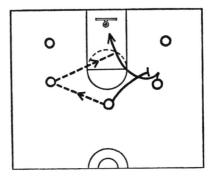

Fig. 112. Screening off ball.

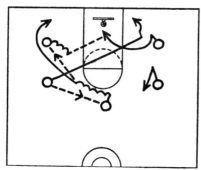

Fig. 113. Cross with deep screen.

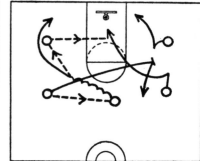

Fig. 114. Cross with outside screen.

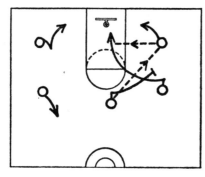

Fig. 115. Screening on ball.

Fig. 116. Cut-away on switch.

In the event two men are placed inside and wide, the wide double post is the result. The placing of men wider allows for maneuvering off screens to shake men loose inside. One-on-one situations are developed where mismatching of men will give an advantage. Due to their speed, smaller men can sometimes be used in the wide double post play with more effective results. As the men are stationed farther apart, naturally the rebounding strength is de-

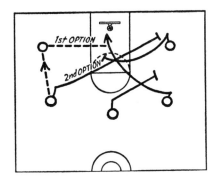 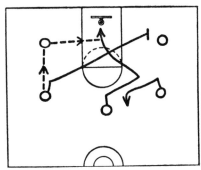

Fig. 117. Side feed with double pick off ball.   Fig. 118. Side feed with cut-away on switch.

creased. Screens effected on and off the ball are efficient in this attack. Splits off the two post men will also be successful.

Angle feeds into the post from the front and side offer good possibilities. It is probable that when defensing this attack the opponents will jam the middle and attempt to force the play and shot outside. Such action will necessitate good outside shooting for your offense. Good passing, screening and cutting options must be employed in this case. Changing of personnel to the various positions will exploit defensive weaknesses and decrease rebounding possibilities. Variations of attack with the open center, such as this provides, creates many opportunities.

The Triple Post

Some coaches have used the triple-post attack successfully. Triple-post plays can be planned and patterned to use personnel wisely if the big man is not available. The placing of the three men close to the basket presents good single and double screen situations. This pattern of attack will also congest the defense, with good shots being available within the fifteen-foot area. Congesting the defense will give them the board advantage on even abilities. The close shooting area, however will compensate for board weak-

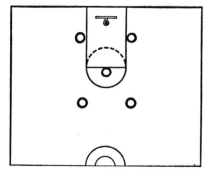

Fig. 119. Triple post system.

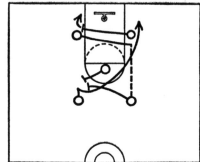

Fig. 120. Double screen.

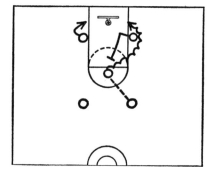

Fig. 121. Blind screen.

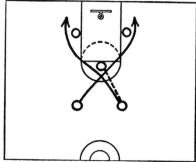

Fig. 122. Split post.

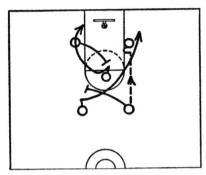

Fig. 123. Cross screen.

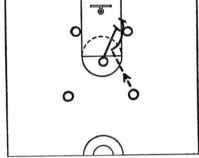

Fig. 124. Jump shot off inside screen.

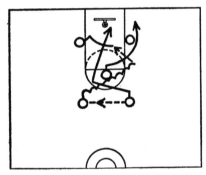

Fig. 125. Dribble across.

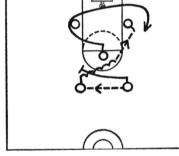

Fig. 126. Center post around.

ness. The medium shot areas are vulnerable to a good attack with the two outside men using screens for good shots.

The triple-post attack can be adjusted well to the various size floors. This is especially true in high school basketball. The three post men should be good shooters close in, good rebounders, and good screeners. The two outside men must be fast, good ball handlers, and exceptional shooters from the free throw lane area. Against a zone defense, the triple post may force the zone to play you inside. If the zone plays you inside, your team's efficiency will increase. With the dual threat against zone and man-to-man, the same attack can be used against both defenses with very little adjusting.

Tandem-Post Attack

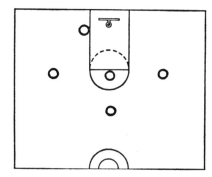

Fig. 127. Tandem post.

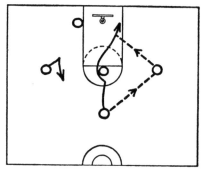

Fig. 128. Run-off opportunity.

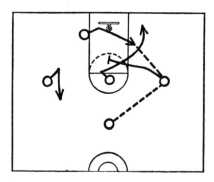

Fig. 129. Side feed with cross screen.

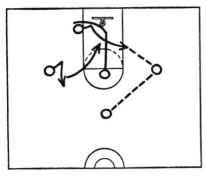

Fig. 130. Exchange of high and low post men.

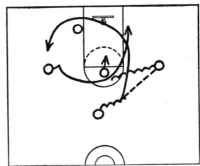

Fig. 131. Three-man weave for drive in or shot off double screen.

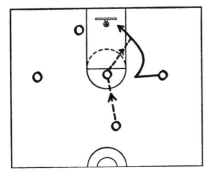

Fig. 132. Back door possibility.

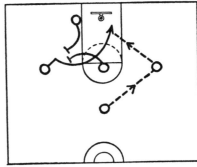

Fig. 133. Double screen.

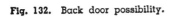

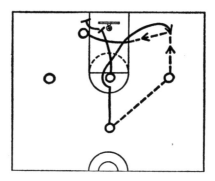

Fig. 134. Run-off with exchange of post
option.

The tandem-post attack was originated and developed by teams that didn't have the expert operator for post play. This system, like the triple post, can be used against both styles of defense with little change. With a high-low post man arrangement, the tandem is similar to the 1-3-1 attack used against many zone defenses. Many good screening and rebounding opportunities are present in this pattern due to strategic placing of personnel. The high-low post exchange of men presents defensive problems. The tandem is also excellent for clear-outs or rub-offs using the high post man.

When adapting this attack to your squad you will need good shooters from a 15-foot distance as well as good rebounding in the high-low post positions. The wing men in the attack must be good shooters with excellent speed to be able to recover. The outside or key man should be an expert feeder, a good driver and a good shooter. This player must be your floor general. He should be able to diagnose the defensive actions quickly and direct the adjustment of your team. Passing the ball quickly in this pattern against a zone will enable you to capitalize on overload possibilities on the side. Sending cutters through the defense, with rub-off opportunities, presents good shots. The rub-off technique will be successful against the zone and man-to-man defense. The simplicity of the plays and the possible quick adaptations to the defense makes the system easier to teach than some of the others.

Open-Center Attack with Flash Pivot

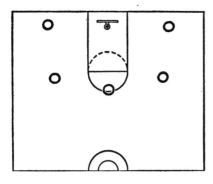

Fig. 135. Placing of men for open center with flash pivot.

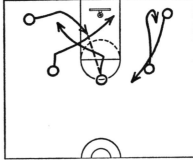

Fig. 136. Three-man weave to open play down center. Attack must start at the center for balance and diversified attack.

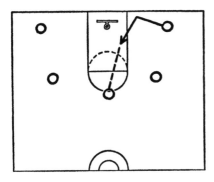

Fig. 137. Flash pivot to get shot.

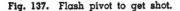

Fig. 138. Flash pivot to split post.

Ken Loeffler, lately of La Salle and Texas A. & M., has experienced a great deal of success with this system. The open center with a flash pivot certainly explores the possibilities of each player. Most pivot offensive attacks concentrate on one or two men. This pattern offers all players a chance to participate as threats. The basic philosophy of this development is to keep the continuity going and maintain pressure on the defense constantly. When all men function well in the operation, all of them can maneuver and participate in the options. If four men are available with passing, screening, and driving abilities, one man can be placed along the base line to play with them. From the base line position, the player can flash into the pivot area to shoot or to set a post for splits or other variations. If only three good outside men are available on your squad, two men can be placed along the base line and alternate moving into the post position.

Any time an advantage can be gained in this offense through height, maneuverability, or defensive weakness, it can be exploited quickly. Good outside shooting abilities are needed to force the defense from clogging middle areas. Give-and-go options, change ups in direction, and double and single screening tactics can be employed in this assault. The center must be kept open. This necessitates teaching men off the ball to move quickly in order to be a constant threat. Absence of the large post man makes feasible the adoption of the open center to utilize abilities of smaller men. Clever maneuvering by smaller men will result in exceptional opportunities. The attack needs to start with the center man to make your pattern strong either way. The corner men must be good rebounders. This system lacks rebounding strength with the open center, but gains some as the larger men are brought into the post play.

The Five-Man Weave

The five-man weave is similar to the open center operation with the flash pivot. The attack differs from the one mentioned in that the baseline men move to the outside instead of the inside. This offensive play can be used effectively with smaller men. It allows many variations for free-lancing opportunities. The action of the

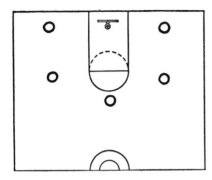

Fig. 139. Placing of men for five-man weave.

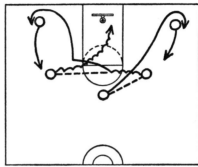

Fig. 140. Continuity of movement off five-man screen against tight screens.

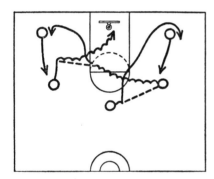

Fig. 141. Continuity of movement off five-man weave against loosening defense.

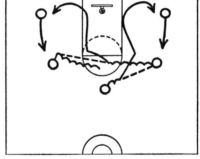

Fig. 142. Continuity of movement off five-man weave against switching defense.

defense dictates the offensive action. The movement in this plan is natural and easy to teach at all age levels. With the center open, emphasis is naturally placed on the inside options. Screened shots can also be set up. Direction toward the basket must be gained with the weave or no inside advantage is acquired.

The attack must begin with the center man. This allows better balance and affords a threat in two directions. The continuity in the weave is sometimes compared to the figure-eight movement. Weaknesses develop in offensive board play unless planned rebounding off the options is considered. This offense can be adjusted quickly and efficiently to defensive changes, unless the defense uses a zone. When the defense plays tight, the offensive screens resulting from this movement will break players free down the middle. This is true only when the opponents do not like to shift men. If the defense elects to release and slide through, a slightly longer pass to the receiver is necessary. As the longer pass is made, approximately six to eight feet, two steps toward the basket by the passer will screen the defensive man as he comes through the alley. This action permits better penetration and offers quicker opportunities at the basket.

In case the defense uses switching tactics, the five-man weave can use the roll-off or the cut-away down the middle. The roll-off or cut-away maneuver comes off a screening situation. When a screen is set, action on a switch allows a step advantage on the screened man. The screener is then open for a quick pass from his teammate after a cross screen. The defense must be spread at all times and the middle of the court kept open for drives toward the basket. Every variation of the five-man weave must get penetration with progress towards the basket. The penetration and advance must be made possible by the screener and the ball handler. Otherwise the defense will be able to force you to take the long shot.

Spectators observe a weave team in operation and marvel at its ability to move and handle the ball. However, the action is kept outside the free throw circle, with limited shot opportunities. The object of the game is to outscore the opponent. Achievement of this goal cannot be reached by merely moving and handling the ball. Penetration must be made inside the defense. Single and double screens can be utilized in this attack and players may be brought into the pivot area for shooting or screening purposes.

The Four-Man Weave with Pivot

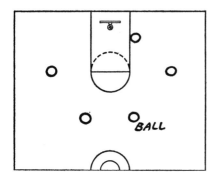

Fig. 143. Placing of men on four-man weave with pivot man on ball.

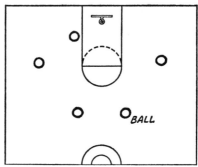

Fig. 144. Placing of men on four-man weave with pivot man off ball.

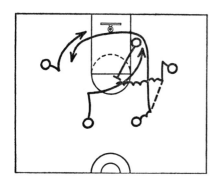

Fig. 145. Double screen option.

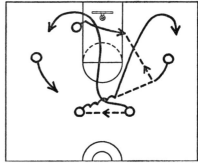

Fig. 146. Movement down center to screen for pivot.

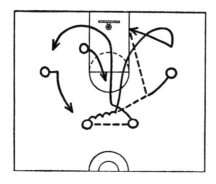

Fig. 147. Change of direction for back door play.

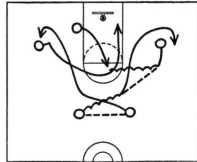

Fig. 148. Four-man weave with high post.

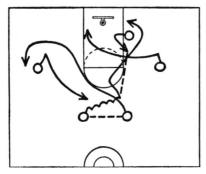

Fig. 149. Split post off the weave.

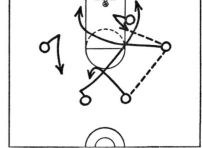

Fig. 150. Outside screen.

If you have a good, big man and four little men, this offense will fit your needs well. The big man can be used to shoot, screen, and hand off, as well as being inside for rebounding. This combination will have to use the pivot man or clear out options to get the inside shot. This is obvious because the post man is in the center of the area which hampers the chance to drive down the middle.

The pivot man can be used for screens with other teammates. Splitting the post will be effective with this type of personnel. When the four men outside are moving, the defense cannot collapse on the pivot man. Good shots are available around the free throw line if the team will penetrate the defense. The pivot man can blind screen front men or players on the side to help his outside men. Double screens can be applied with the post man to create more pressure on the defense.

Good ball handling and maneuvering are essential for this offense. Change of direction maneuvers used by the corner men with the post man high or off the ball will create openings. The writer once saw a high school team use this system with a 7-foot pivot man. The four outside men averaged 5 feet 7 inches in height. The small men would weave and then expertly lob a high pass into the seven footer. He would then hold the ball aloft with arms extended above his head. The defenders, after attempting to reach the ball with several jumps, would tire and the over-sized pivot player would make the basket without much opposition. The system was more effective with such a tall man when the narrow free-throw lane was in effect. Today's widened lane would make this play harder to work. The big man is less efficient with the wide lane unless he can maneuver well. The "goon" has been equalized somewhat with the change of rules. Either of the front men can start this attack with equal results when starting the play in the weave and post attack.

The Free-Lance Attack

Many coaches contend it is a waste of time to spend practice on plays and options, only to have the players forget to run them in a game. To these coaches, the teaching process consists of plenty of scrimmage, plus the experience acquired in games. It is easy to understand the confusion in play when there is no organized attack. It is also true that a team should not be too mechanized or stereotyped with pattern play. From these two statements we might deduce that a combination of the two types of play would be the solution. A team must have organization and pattern play to keep good floor balance. It is also necessary to open lanes and keep the defensive men occupied. However, when the defense gambles and creates an opening, the offensive unit should capitalize on it, permitting free-lance play.

In pattern play, you must have your team run the plays many times with and without opposition. By repetition and game situations, as well as many hours of drill, a team can develop organized play. Many teams use the free-lance style of play using the theory of "learning by doing." When no drills are used to correct mistakes, the same mistakes occur in the offense. These mistakes must be corrected before they become habitual. In small communities where five boys mature and play together, the free-lance play becomes successful through repeated play and familiarity of actions. Changes in defensive tactics or other surprises effected by the defense will certainly disorganize and confuse the free-lance team.

It is always easy for anyone to escape responsibility by making excuses for weaknesses in play. When a coach does his job well with many hours of planning and hard work, it is possible to realize an objective. Consequently, it is possible to teach pattern and free-lance. With many variations of defense being used today, a counter attack must go into action quickly. Free-lance teams operating without balance and objective attack will always be in trouble with equal competition. Basketball with its scientific ideas of play being advanced has now isolated the "get what you can" offense. A team must have organization with free-lance opportunities to achieve success consistently.

Offensive Rebound Organization

Regardless of the offensive attack employed, some planning and drill must be achieved to guarantee effective offensive rebounding. This is necessary to get the desired second and third shot. On each play or option, planned position will afford good rebounding. Triangular position of three men near the basket will help to achieve this. The triangle is formed when one man is placed on each side of the basket with a third man in front of the basket. The defensive team attempts to form the triangle also with a position advantage. Equal matching by the offense must take place if the second shot is to be secured.

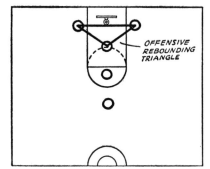 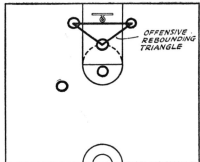

Fig. 151. The ideal positions for offensive rebound organization.

Fig. 152. The practical positions for offensive rebound organization.

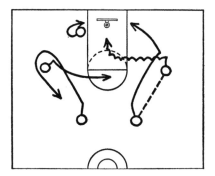

Fig. 153. Play option to illustrate this position for offensive rebound organization.

In addition to the rebounding triangle, one man can be placed at the free throw line to retrieve the long rebound. The fifth man on the team should be between the free throw circle and mid-court for defensive assignment. When the movement is planned to achieve this position of men, the offensive opportunities will increase. The defense will be forced to fight for board control. The majority of teams attempt to place their big men inside on both offense and defense to help board coverage. In case the small man is taken inside, he must know how to get position for effective board play.

In the event the offense surrenders the boards without a contest, their defensive playing time will increase. You must take care not to overplay the boards with four and five men rebounding. If you do, you will be vulnerable to the fast break. Three men in the triangle with one man at the free throw lane should suffice for rebounding opportunities. All necessary maneuvering by the offense to gain position on the board will have to be done while the ball is in flight toward the basket. After the ball has hit the basket or bankboard, it is too late to get position. The offensive player must fight to gain position between his opponent and the basket. He is of no value behind the opponent unless the opponent is out of position or weak in the techniques of rebounding. The ball can be stolen easily if not properly protected by the man in position. Practice time should emphasize rebounding with every option having a rebounding triangle when or immediately after the shot is attempted. Rebounding organization of both phases of the game is a must and should be planned well and thoroughly as an important part of the game.

Defensive Balance Off the Offensive Attack

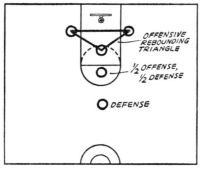
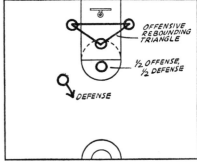

Fig. 154. The ideal position for defensive balance during the attack.   Fig. 155. The practical positions for defensive balance during the attack.

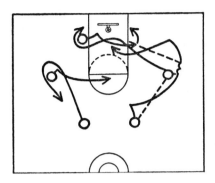

Fig. 156. Option to illustrate this
position for recovery.

With the popular use of the fast break by many teams, your team should be able to adjust quickly from offense to defense. Without proper balance and recovery of position, your team will certainly be vulnerable to the fast break. There is nothing easier to score than a fast break basket when the defense does not recover. The fast break fears no defensive setup, as it can hit before the defense is ready. You can prevent your opponents from capitalizing on the fast break off the defensive board by careful planning of your offense. This theory is associated with offensive rebounding organization and must have sufficient strength to combat the quick attack.

The three and one-half offensive rebounding pattern with a one and one-half defensive recovery is necessary for good protection off the patterns. The player at the free throw line will get a large number of rebounds. This man will also be able to play defensive position. When the offense has two men in these positions, with the other men able to recover quickly, the opponent will have less opportunity to break away. Boards must be contested with at least three men. By beating the opponents on the board and contesting the pass out, you can delay the fast break. If the opponents never fast break, you can compensate somewhat on defensive balance.

Even then your team must not become careless and allow your opponents easy chances. Careful planning and practice in defensive recovery, along with position in the offensive attack, is a good guarantee against humiliation. Otherwise, if your plans do not cover this phase of the game, the score can increase rapidly against your team.

What System Will Succeed?

Most of the systems discussed in this chapter have been successful. The success of any system depends on good personnel and excellent execution of fundamental play. Although most systems are copied and used, there is room for improvement in some phases. Even new ideas and systems can be introduced into the game. You will need to possess imagination and courage to try something different. This ingenuity will help the game to improve, advance, and increase in popularity. One of the great thrills of coaching is to improve a play or to inaugurate a new idea and see it work successfully. Without this type of thinking to improve the game, basketball would not be as interesting and popular as it is today. In spite of the many criticisms of the game, basketball remains the most popular game in attendance and participation. This would not be the case if old theories had been accepted and not improved. Perhaps 10 years from now some of the popular styles of attack today will be obsolete and new ideas and systems will add interest to the game. That is the challenge offered to all young men in the coaching profession. There is no doubt but that they will meet the challenge. With the added abilities of youngsters and more interest in the game, basketball will continue toward more progressive efficiency and supply more thrills to participants and spectators.

• 3 •

Achieving Offensive Objectives Through Break-down Drills and Patterns

----

Introduction and Objectives

With the fundamentals stressed and a selection of the planned system made, begin teaching the offense by explaining the system and your objectives in developing the offensive attack. In this development, it is advantageous to take certain phases of the attack and build up systematically a total offense which will involve all of your plays and strategy.

Explain the purpose of your plan at the blackboard before introducing it to your squad on the floor. Films of previous games will also help the squad to understand the reasoning behind certain maneuvers and patterns. By doing this, the retention of floor balance and driving lanes will usually be greater. The effect of two- and three-man plays on the ball, as well as learning to play off the ball, can best be shown by films or by drawing. Many times players off the ball feel they have to get in the act and as a result spoil the efforts of the other team members executing a play. It will also help them see the need for rebounding position and defensive

83

balance, and to understand the basic requirements of the system. This is an important part in selling your system to the squad. Many of the squad members will ask good questions and your answers must be convincing to help them believe your ideas will work. Often team members will run a play which will be better and more efficient than the one you asked them to run. If this happens, do not be too proud to acknowledge a boy's thinking, but include it in the possible variations of the attack. The fact that such an attack has had previous success will help in selling it to your squad. Sometimes you may want to vary it a little, explaining to the squad that the pattern is in the trial stage. It is also a good idea to have a new play or pattern occasionally to fool the opposition. If the new play works, it will have tremendous effect on the squad and build greater confidence in the coach; the fun of fooling the opponent is gratifying to all concerned.

Breakdown Drills

These drills should be a part of the play that might ensue in actual game situations. Every drill should apply to some phase of the game to teach desired results better. Any drill that does not contribute to fundamental proficiency or game potential is wasted completely. Drills can be established to take care of basic offensive needs and to help improve weaknesses. Breakdown drills should include all phases of your attack. Introducing these drills without opposition will work out the details and timing. After there is a good understanding of these drills, add opposition to get the game situation. Such breakdown drills as rebounding, fast break, and others of your system can be used successfully.

When the defense is added to the breakdown drills, the situations and the reactions of the drills can better be established in the thoughts and actions of your players. With fewer players involved, more repetition of the play can be given. Defensive work can also be stressed off these breakdown drills. The three-man weave or plays involving post men with front or side feeds from teammates are the most popular type drills to help build the over-all system of play. As the patterns are developed through these means, the fourth and fifth man can be added to the drill to present the whole attack and acquaint all five players with their responsibility in the attack. As the players learn their jobs, the offensive patterns will develop, and the team will begin to take advantage of whatever openings the defensive alignment offers. Much time and patience must be allowed on these drills to teach the proper execution and movement necessary.

Patterns

Distinct patterns bring about better organization of play. With the teaching of patterns, however, you should be careful not to stereotype or mechanize so that play is forced. This situation will generally result in successful defensive play against you, as well as the possibilities of mistakes occurring through forced play. As movement of men and ball occurs with screens, the defense is forced to make movements and adjustments to allow for scoring opportunities on the part of the offense. Depending on your philosophy and pattern play, free-lance can either be allowed by you or your players may not capitalize on many scoring opportunities. Initiative may be developed through free-lance play while it will be curtailed in a designed strict-pattern offense. Practice on patterns should begin the first day of practice and run every day. Even with all the time spent on these patterns, youngsters will have mental lapses and forget their assignments. The only answer to this problem is repetition of drill and pattern until the players can do a good job with your offensive plan.

When introducing the style of attack and the patterns to be used, you should place the boys in their respective positions on the floor and explain to them your reason for wanting them in that particular position. This is what is generally called the skeleton attack without defensive opposition. The types of passes and the maneuvers used in the play should be given when the pattern is introduced. The play must be identified with a number or a name so that all players and coaches will know what is being discussed and can understand what is taking place in the discussion of the play. When the play is introduced and used in practice or games it must have some key or signal to inform everyone on the team to know what play is being started by the quarterbacks, so called because they start all the set plays from the outside. Some teams call numbers or use the hand to designate the play to be used. Other teams use certain passes or ball signals to tell the other players what play is desired. It is always best to mix the plays and patterns well to keep the defense off balance. The same play used too often is much easier to stop. Sometimes small changes, such as position of men, will help to keep the defense off balance.

Skeleton Patterns

The plays and patterns can now be practiced without opposition. Fewer plays with efficient execution will generally be better than many plays poorly executed. The five players involved in the pattern should go through these plays about half speed to give them the initial feel of the execution. After this has been tried with confidence, full speed should then be the rule in running these plays. During the running of these patterns in skeleton form, check on footwork, timing, screens, floor balance, and other things that are important in making the play successful. All of these patterns are practiced first on the assumption that a certain type of man-for-man defense will be used. Variations of defense need to be shown early so adjustments can be made early and practiced. A zone defense will offer different problems and needs to be treated differently from an offensive angle. In most cases, the maneuver being attempted will involve players on the ball. Such change-ups as roll-offs, cut-aways, trailers, and other possibilities must be shown to the team to acquaint them with what they will have to do in case the defense adjusts to the play with a different tactic.

These new possibilities require constant thinking and good reaction time on the part of the players to adjust quickly to any surprise element. If there is no maneuver for the defensive change up, then the play slows down and becomes ineffective. In this case the defense forces you to regroup for another attempt which results in a slowing of the attack. For every movement of the defense, the offense should have a counter-movement to carry the attack to the opponents and maintain pressure on them without delay. All of the plays should be introduced individually and practiced one at a time until the squad can run them well. Rhythm and continued movement must accompany each play in this skeleton type play. When the plays have been practiced to the extent that the boys do them well and understand the objective, the opposition should be added to introduce the game situation possibilities that will result from the attempted offensive plays and patterns.

Patterns with Defense

With the addition of the defense, the offensive team now gets the practice of actual operation of the patterns. This is best introduced with half-court practice. The defense will have to be orthodox for the plays to work as they are designed. This will necessitate the defensive unit being instructed to play the man and not the play, or confusion and lack of confidence can exist and become a negative factor. With the practice of each play, work must be continued until the play experiences some success. Corrections and checkouts must be made at this time. Insistence on finer details of the play is very important at this stage of the instruction period. Sloppy execution allowed to progress will be harder to correct later in the stage of introduction and practice. As the practice of plays continues, assistants or other players can help you make the necessary check-outs for successful execution.

After the team has a basic understanding of the patterns against the defense you are most apt to face during the season, variations of defensive play can be introduced to acquaint the team with the offensive adjustments necessary to counteract defensive moves. Again, most of this early play must be worked against defenses with man-to-man principle. Any zone defense must be treated differently. Such variations as switching, double teaming, pressing, sagging, and "swivel heads" must be shown with the movement necessary to counteract the defensive move. In other words, the defense must be kept honest at all times and not permitted to overplay or gamble with success.

All of the half-court practice should stress offensive and defensive development. Much time must be spent daily in working on the details and practicing the patterns with all the possibilities. When your team has practiced under these conditions and operates with confidence and success, then other phases of the game must be coordinated with this plan to cover all the necessary phases needed for a good attack. Good shooting areas must be impressed on all team members so they will know when they have a good shot to attempt. An effort to get the good second shot must be made. Proper positioning of men at the time of the first shot can be established for follow-up opportunities. With all these factors explained and practiced under game situations, your players will react more quickly and recognize the possibilities when they occur in the game. Proper planning and proper coaching will insure this in most cases. If your opponent's play contains an element of surprise, you must help your team with proper diagnosis and instruction from the bench. Sound advice and help will be more beneficial than the usual fight talk made to spur your team on.

You Will Need Patience

Even with the strong emphasis placed on pattern practice, with and without opposition, the boys will forget some of the details necessary for successful operation. Many times coaches wonder about the mental capacity of youngsters who have practiced the patterns many hours and, in spite of the time and drill, forget their assignment. This condition is part of the process of learning and the patterns must be practiced and repeated over and over to impress and to teach the proper movements. When the players of your team seem to have forgotten what to do with their patterns or certain situations, perhaps the play has only been rehearsed 800 times when possibly 1,000 rehearsals would have made it a successful play. Time, patience, and an adequate understanding of young men all help when the previously mentioned situation occurs in basketball.

• 4 •

Effective Scrimmage, Checkouts, and Statistics

When the basic objectives of the system have been explained to the squad, necessary practice on skeleton plays should follow. Opposition can then be added as the next step in the teaching process to coordinate these essentials into half-court scrimmage. This will acquire the experience necessary in running play patterns with game possibilities. Inasmuch as most of the offensive action takes place in front court, the teaching of all the possibilities in front court will give better results. Because of the experience needed through proper practice, half-court scrimmage will help to develop efficiency in the operation. Half-court play will have to be practiced at full speed to gain the most from it. The defense can be allowed to make adjustments necessary to stop the chance to score. All mistakes must be corrected immediately; they must not be allowed to become habit.

It is sound teaching procedure in the early stage of learning to stop the play when the defense gains possession of the ball or when a basket is scored. This process will allow more time for repetition in teaching the scrimmage pattern. Only one play should be practiced at a time at the beginning of half-court scrimmage. This method will enable you to stress the technical details of play. It will also help to impress the players with the need to develop correct pattern maneuvers. Any opportunity to free-lance or take advantage of the defense to score quickly should be encouraged and taught all players at this time. The free-lance maneuvers will develop only as fast as the players are able to recognize and adjust to the situation as it occurs. Any late recognition and adjustment will not succeed as the defense will be able to recover and play the possibility.

The Defense Can Start a Fast Break

If your team uses the fast break, the defense can make the first pass out after ball recovery. A follow-up with the complete fast break pattern can be made later as the team progresses. This action will help keep the offense alert to the possibilities of attack. The need for good defensive floor balance off the offensive attack can also be stressed. If these possibilities are not employed, there is often a tendency on the part of the players to loaf at this time. The habit may be carried into your game play and hurt your chances to win. Practicing this way helps to develop alertness and quick recovery when your attack changes to defense with a score or loss of ball on a shot attempt. If your team does not employ the fast break style of play, then practice on these details will not apply.

Full-Court Scrimmage

When progress has been made with half-court drill and the players run the plays with confidence and precision, full-court scrimmage should follow to coordinate back court play with front court play. This phase of development moves into the objectives planned for your over-all play according to the system used. By using the step by step process of teaching and building an attack, you may now see the end product of your time investment and planning.

No doubt many rough spots will appear in the early scrimmages. The primary purpose of full-court play is to detect these weaknesses, and to learn what has to be corrected through other drills and play.

Such defensive tactics as full-court press and the semi-press can be introduced, and the attack given to the squad which will best counteract the defensive strategy. Fast break tactics and control work can also be emphasized as play progresses, and improvement in play justifies the new information.

As play develops and the season progresses, the question of how much to scrimmage becomes a problem. You will need to have enough full-court scrimmages for proper conditioning and learning. The possibility of too much scrimmage may result in destroying a boy's interest and desire to play. It is always wise to regulate properly your full-court scrimmage so the squad members will want to continue after you decide to conclude the practice. Consider it a dangerous sign when you release the boys from practice and they run to the showers as though they were thrilled the practice is over. To have to encourage them to leave the floor indicates their desire is still present.

The combination of break-down drills used with half-court and full-court scrimmage must be varied wisely as the needs and results show. This method will be more successful than many long scrimmages with the philosophy of learning to play by playing continuously. It will also be necessary to select your best working combination early and let them play together. This will acquaint them with each other and their particular habits of play.

Checkouts Needed on Scrimmage

Along with fundamental observations certain checkouts should be made during all scrimmages. With a close scrutiny of action and proper corrections, the team will advance much faster and reach its peak with greater efficiency.

Footwork

Angle running, which makes the job of the defense more difficult, develops proper footwork maneuvering. It consists of quick maneuvers to change-up in speed or direction. The dividends will be much better in basketball play with angle running than with circle running, which is easier to defense. When a boy is properly taught the fundamentals of angle running, attention must be given to the following:

1. Proper footwork and body balance should be presented along with head and shoulder fakes.
2. Proper use of speed must be taught so the change-up can be used successfully.
3. The opportune time to use the change-up should be given.
4. Proper placing of the driving foot can be shown to secure better results.
    a. When running to a player's right side, the drive must be made off the right foot with the left foot angled to change direction.
    b. When running to a player's left side, the drive must be made off the left foot with the right foot angled to change direction.
    c. The cut must never be made with the inside foot as this action reduces speed and results in slight circle running.

A good halfback in football needs this same action to cut sharply to use his blockers. When angle running is mastered, screens can be set more effectively and defensive men can be out-maneuvered more easily. Such action enables your player to gain the advantage necessary for a good shot.

Proper footwork must be practiced to evade a tight defensive man who is contesting every move to prohibit the pass from getting to your inside men. Verbal instruction will never be sufficient. Practice and checkouts in scrimmage are the means to this end. The proper footwork technique must be mastered by your post men or they will not know the act of getting free to receive the pass. Angle running, change of direction, and faking are the skills necessary to outwit the defense.

Screens

Proper positioning for screens and the legal execution of them must be checked. If the screens are taught illegally, your players will have fouls called on them; this will be confusing and hard to correct without practice. When the screens are set effectively to check the opponent's progress, the defense will have more problems and the offense will experience more opportunities. Multiple screens, if used, must be checked according to the position of the men. Various types of screens, such as set, moving, and multiple, may be used in the same attack. Proper positioning for roll-off and cut-away tactics with trailer possibilities must also be checked in scrimmage when the defense permits that opportunity. The coach should make early and frequent checks on the way his players execute their screens. This will help to instill in the players confidence in the system.

Floor Balance

In any organized pattern attack, it is necessary that floor balance be maintained. Proper positioning of players is required for good balance to keep the opponent's defensive play spread. Many times in the early stage of scrimmage, players will congest in areas and clog driving lanes or stop the chance to maneuver well. In your checking process, players off the ball must be watched. Have them maneuver properly to keep their men occupied and insist they maintain their position on the floor. Often during scrimmage, play can be stopped when there is congestion, and this important point shown more effectively to the players. They can readily see the situation and be impressed with the need to keep some distance apart. Films of early scrimmages are effective teaching aids in helping to get the offensive play started correctly.

Statistics

Statistics serve a very important purpose in modern day basketball. Many consistent facts can be revealed concerning details of your team's play. Accurate statistics will identify flaws and strong points existing in scrimmage and in games. Memory and visual retention are not sufficient for such evaluation of shot areas, passing, rebounding, violations, and defensive play. To have these statistics in black and white helps to defend your purposes in determining specific drills that must be used to increase efficiency in your team's play. Statistics are also very helpful in determining proper personnel to fill the respective positions on the team. These accurate records help to chart the way for more effective play as the season progresses. Without them the coach has no way of planning progress wisely.

Shot Charts

Shot charts will show whether your offense favors the right or left side of the floor. These are also very good in determining the proper balance in the attack. They also help to pinpoint where the offense is able to get shots, and thus determine the penetration of the attack. The number of shots taken in a prescribed amount of play is important in determining the tempo of the shooting pattern. Shot percentages are also very important to know. Your opponent's shot chart will inform you of your defensive play and help your team's efforts more effectively.

Rebounds

If games are to be won consistently, the bankboards must be controlled. Rebounding statistics will help you check position and proper blocking out for offensive and defensive triangles. These statistics will also reveal the boys who can do the best job for you when the ball is shot at either basket. The charts will prove the strength and weakness of your rebounding. This information is important to determine the need for drill and emphasis on strengthening this part of your game. Some boys are natural rebounders, but most of the players participating today need a lot of work in that fundamental of the game. The writer recalls an experience when his team played a strong Kentucky team in the Sugar Bowl Tournament. We were beaten badly on the boards and lost the game. Such men as Hagen, Linville, Ramsey and others on the Kentucky team proved we were weak on rebounding. Statistics also showed an overwhelming balance on the boards in Kentucky's favor. Because of this, we returned home and taught basic, simple fundamentals in rebounding. The team became more efficient because of our work as the season progressed. Without these statistics, and the good lesson we received, our rebounding could have remained a weak point in our play.

Bad Passes and Violations

Offensive mistakes caused by bad passes and violations will certainly offset your team's opportunity to score. It is always difficult to win games when a team loses possession of the ball before getting a shot. Every bad pass or violation that results in loss of possession naturally costs your team a chance to score two points and gives your opponents the chance to gain two points. These statistics will help you determine your poor ball handlers, poor passers and violators. The record will be convincing to your players, and the personnel weak in these important fundamentals of the game will react to instruction and increased work with added interest. It is most discouraging to have your team lose the ball by sloppy passing or poor ball handling. A double dribble or a traveling violation is just as costly before the scoring chance presents itself. The better shots are always obtained by a team that is strong in these fundamentals. During a closely contested game, any one of these mistakes can easily result in your team's losing. Conversely, a team strong in these points will win more than its share of the close ones.

Defensive Balance

In an effort to stimulate greater desire to play defense, you should keep this record on each player along with the other statistical data. The defensive balance phase of statistical records is nothing more than the results of matching men during scrimmage. The balance of points on the majority side constitutes the defensive balance. In other words, when men are assigned to play against each other it becomes a battle to determine the victor with an advantage of points scored. There are many factors that contribute to better defensive play and this could be one. This method is not foolproof, as switch offs to pick up a man in position to score may result in a player having a negative balance. The fact that the boys on your team know these statistics are being kept will spur them on to greater defensive performance.

In most cases, youngsters are thrilled with the offensive part of the game. The satisfaction seems to lie in being able to score and get the headlines. The less glamorous part of the game, defense, is hard work and not as much fun for the players or as noticeable to the public. Nevertheless, it is a very important part of the game. The defensive balance record will offer an incentive to your players to aspire to greater things offensively, while impressing them with the need for defensive play.

• 5 •

Successful Team Morale and Conditioning

Team Morale

Regardless of the proficiency of the team in the execution of fundamentals and skills, all this will be for naught if the team does not possess good spirit and high morale. Basketball, probably more than any other sport, requires teamwork of the highest degree. All of the ability that might exist within a group of boys will not lead to success unless they work in harmony as a team unit. Average ability teams will sometimes defeat teams with outstanding individual ability, because they work as a unit to achieve a common purpose. The same spirit that needs to exist on a regular starting unit, will need to be present among the substitutes to provide for over-all harmony and team work.

Any program of athletics needs the cooperative support of everyone concerned. This will include the administration, the alumni, the townspeople, the student body, the parents, the coaching staff, and the team. It can never be a one-way street which allows only for "front runners" that exist only when winning. The coach plays an important part in helping through public relations—and especially through winning—to coordinate the program with all these

97

groups. The philosophy of the coach regarding the importance of education, and sports activity, and the related values of sportsmanship and ethics, will be instrumental in contributing to an outstanding program.

Probably the greatest asset needed by all groups in the program is the courage or the desire to excel or to win. This trait must exist, and winning must be the objective at all times. Caution must be taken, however, that winning is not placed above every other value; a win-at-any-cost attitude should not be assumed. Any boy on a team who doesn't play to win every game, misses one of the greatest things in life. Of course, this desire to win must take into account the acceptance of the rules of the game. Young men should never be taught to take advantage of the rules to win. This applies to the phrase, "win at all costs," an attitude which sometimes goes to the extent of considering it permissible to injure outstanding opponents. Cheating, in any form, can never be condoned in any athletic contest. Many times spectators will remark that it is too bad that both teams can't win. There is nothing less American than this attitude. If this was the accepted philosophy of all, there would be no challenge, no score would need to be kept, and after a friendly contest everyone could go home with nothing having been proved.

When a boy plays his best and plays to win, there might be slight consolation even in defeat if he, in his opinion, has done the best he could. This consolation, however, must never be a complete feeling of satisfaction with his performance. He must always attempt to improve his play in every game. There is no time in athletics, the participant being willing of course, when the player ceases to learn. Even professional players, after 15 years of playing, maintain they learn something in each game. When a boy has played to the top of his capabilities in a losing cause, he may still walk away with pride and confidence in his ability. In an outmanned contest where defeat is inevitable, a boy playing his best can be hurt by being accused of letting down.

A boy not playing his best will always be plagued with the feeling of wondering what the outcome might have been if he had played his best. There is no place in athletics for the boy who doesn't want to win, and who only plays with a partial interest in the result. You may have to endure these boys occasionally in order to have sufficient personnel to make the game possible. You will prefer the boy who comes to play to win, however, rather than the youngster who plays simply to model his suit.

Tradition

Tradition plays an important part in establishing good morale. High standards of competition, and achievement by previous teams, provide a wholesome challenge for all who follow and help to instill in them the desire to achieve also. No one wants to be a bad apple in the barrel and each boy will strive to reach pinnacles of success that otherwise he would not try to reach if tradition were forgotten. Goals of achievement must be established and every effort made to make the most of the possibilities and talent to achieve these goals.

Congeniality

If a team is to succeed, all members of the group must be congenial and learn to get along with each other. Tempers will flare occasionally and feelings will be hurt, but these situations should be kept to a minimum and straightened out through understanding and equal treatment. Congenial conditions will generally be present when each boy, through equal opportunity and fair treatment, knows the whole situation. Then in this way each player will know that he has the same chance. If another boy is participating ahead of him, he will work harder to replace that boy and still thrill with the success of his teammate and the team. Team success must always be placed ahead of individual glory. Successful teams gain recognition for themselves and individual members. Individualists, who may be successful in certain skills and gain recognition for it, will in most cases never experience the thrills that accompany a team championship.

Psychology Is Necessary

It is important that a coach be somewhat of a psychologist and understand human nature. Different personalities comprise the group and each will have to be handled separately, yet be treated with fairness and firmness. As far as privileges are concerned, all members of the group should have the same opportunity. To make exceptions, unless for a good reason and explained to other squad members, will generally result in trouble. As the coach, you will have to treat each boy's problem as it arises. Some youngsters have to be scolded and driven, while others need encouragement and leadership. You will need to be friendly with your squad to the extent that they have confidence in you, but the friendliness of the boy should never reach the point when he may take advantage of it and also of you. Firm discipline, understanding, and respect must be established and maintained between both parties. Once you make a statement or a rule, be sure that neither will have a double set of values. Goals can be realized better when both parties know what is expected and desired.

A coach should never hold a grudge against a boy or his parents. Many times parents become concerned because their son does not make the team or play as much as they think he should. In most cases the boy in this situation will have faith in the coach and maintain his loyalty to the coach and team if he knows he has been given a fair chance to make good. Because of your fair treatment, he will defend you and be loyal to you as his coach—even against his own family. Parents should be given the courtesy of an audience with you, if they desire, and all factors should be presented by you to prove your case. Many times accurate statistics will help you convince the parents of your thinking and actions. If you do not convince them, however, and they spread gossip about your inabilities to teach, you should never punish their boy for their acts. If the boy agrees with his parents, then he should be removed from the squad.

If the team has a losing streak on, or if a boy makes a costly mistake that might mean losing a game, good common sense must be used. Neither a boy nor the squad should be publicly criticized by a coach in either of these cases. The young men playing for you feel just as bad as you do when the team loses. This is the time to pat them on the back and collectively work harder to attain improvement. Glory and prestige will always accompany success.

Sometimes it is a short experience and can change to severe criticism after a loss. These are the experiences you may expect as a coach. All talk and criticism of the team should be confined to the team and not given to the fans to try and make you look good in defeat as well as victory. You must always remember you and the squad win together and you lose together.

Your Influence Is Important

No one in a youngster's life will have more influence on his character and ideals than his coach. In many cases this is true even beyond the family ties. A youngster will often seek the guidance and counsel of his coach even before he seeks that from his mother or father. The coach is better informed of the boy's background and conditions than any other faculty member and can qualify to help the youngster better because of it. To play together, work together, travel, eat and sleep with youngsters gives the coach a closer association with and better understanding of boys than any other people in the teaching profession. Sometimes you will have to be a father, a psychologist, a sociologist, a banker and, indeed, a friend to all of the boys you have the pleasure of working with. Confidence in them will lead to confidence in you. Because of this situation, your standards of moral and ethical conduct must always be the highest, and thus beyond question. In this case, it is imperative that you teach and impress by being a good solid example and believe in the better things in life.

Education Is Important Too

As the young men you have worked with graduate and continue their education and become good citizens, much joy is experienced by the coach who feels that somewhere along the way, he may have contributed something in their lives to possibly make them better men. In these experiences, you must never lose sight of the importance of an education to the boy. Education, on any level, must come first and athletics second. When athletic achievement becomes more important to a boy than educational achievement, the youngster involved will have a false sense of values and will be in trouble. Athletics as a secondary activity will help many young boys to gain the first objective of a good sound education, and at the same time will help make the educational process more enjoyable. The day of the "athletic bum" has gone and the person looking for the free ride has no place in our educational program. Many boys are saved in education by the athletic program, and all the money spent saving one or two boys a year is wisely invested. There is no doubt but that a youngster interested and engaged in wholesome sports activity will have less time and interest to explore the alleys of juvenile delinquency. The boy who is content to do just enough in his studies to get by, will always be on thin ice and play the same way. This player is usually the type who doesn't come through when the chips are down. Education, like athletics, must be 100 per cent participation to gain the most from it. Educational policies must exist which demand a certain level of academic proficiency to make students eligible to participate in athletics. Moreover, you can help youngsters with better counseling and guidance because of it.

Conditioning

The writer once heard an outstanding college coach give the following reply to the question of whether or not he would try to coach his own son when the latter was in high school: "I'll never try to coach the boy. When he comes under the tutelage of the high school coach, he will do what his coach wants him to do. But, if that coach doesn't get him in good physical condition to play, I will." That statement certainly sums up the importance of good physical conditioning. If a young boy is going to meet the physical demands placed on his body by the game of basketball, or any other athletic contest, then he needs to protect that body by proper health habits and conditioning. By doing this, the athlete will protect somewhat the vital organs and systems of the body at the time of competition, which will also help him in later life. The task of proper conditioning is a cooperative one on the part of the player and coach. The coach can do much to accomplish this, but he must also have help from the team member to achieve the conditioning necessary.

Guides and Counsel Will Help

Certain guides and suggestions must be made by you to help these athletes with their thinking in regard to good conditioning principles. Under daily practice procedures, physical stamina can be increased and helped by you. Other good living habits must also be emphasized at this time. The question arises of establishing hard, fast rules for the players. If rules are made and everyone knows what is expected of him, the rules should be enforced. If suggestions are offered and evidence of these suggestions being ignored exists, then measures to correct the offenders should be taken. The question of driving or leading must be decided on. A youngster can be placed on his honor and the responsibility might be accepted by him. When this situation occurs, there is no need of policing or spying on the boy. Many times this confidence in the boy will result in more desire to do the right thing and other checks can be made in regard to his physical training. Such checks as daily weight charts and statistics of scrimmage, along with keen observation of the practice and game sessions, become the measuring factors. When the athlete is aware of these possible checks, he is less apt to break training.

It should be general philosophy that a boy reports for a sport because of his interest and his desire to succeed. If the athlete assumes the attitude that he will pay the price to play well and work hard to achieve success, he will do nothing to harm his body or reduce his opportunity and ability to excel. If a boy wants to experience the pain that accompanies poor training habits, then he is the one that will have to endure the pain and not the coach. If the pain is extreme enough to cause great suffering, the athlete will generally have learned the hard way, which is often the effective way. Of course, you will always have the one who wants to be different by breaking training rules, and who believes he is fooling other people. In reality, he is only fooling and hurting himself.

What to Eat

Some coaches prescribe dietary measures that should not apply at all times. Some coaches allow only certain foods at all meals.

The author remembers one coach who would feed his boys only poached eggs and toast on the day of the game. Many of his boys got so tired of this menu they hated for the day of a game to come. Variety in this situation would have certainly been the spice of life. A sound conditioning program in regard to foods can be achieved with a good variety of foods chosen wisely and alternated somewhat so that monotony at the table does not move into your program. On the high school level, a boy will usually do well if he eats what his mother prepares for him. There is nothing like Mom's cooking and guidance for a good balanced diet. However, a youngster will need guidance when he has to select his food, since too many times the eyes will deceive the stomach. This can be provided by the coach or the trainer properly educating the players on what is good for them to eat during the season. A good, balanced diet with variations will always help you keep good team morale when traveling. Typically, youngsters will know what agrees with them and what foods are good for them.

What Not to Eat

There must of necessity be a policy for all participants in athletics to abstain from the use of harmful substances. This would include refraining from the use of alcohol, tobacco, and harmful drugs. It is our opinion that young athletes will also be better off without the use of tea and coffee or other mild stimulants. There is no question that alcohol, tobacco, and drugs have no place in an athlete's program. This has been proven beyond a doubt in all tests that have been made for this purpose. Tea and coffee, as mild stimulants, may put extra strain on the vital organs in addition to the emotional strains that accompany the participation in any sports competition. Juices and fruits will supply the quick energy that some contend they get from the sugar used in some beverages. Overstimulation, which might be caused by the mentioned harmful substances, is not good for youngsters. Many older athletes condition their body through the use of some of these substances and get good performance in spite of it. The question that arises is would they perform much better and enjoy good health longer in life if they didn't use them? There is no question but that their performance would be better, and that at 40 their health would be better, without the use of the harmful substances. It is always a sad sight to see a former great and well-conditioned athlete become a picture of dissipation through the use of harmful substances. Athletes' health, reaction time, and performance will be much better without these substances.

Regularity Is Essential

It is apparent that regularity should be practiced in eating, sleeping and elimination. It is bad practice to eat between meals, as the digestive system gets no rest and hunger becomes a lost thing. Through regular eating habits the body functions can be better adjusted and regulated. An active athlete needs a great deal of rest. The season is generally long and many games are played over short periods of time. It is recommended, by most coaches, that youngsters get at least 10 hours sleep each night to maintain the pace. The hours of sleep before midnight are often regarded as more important than those after midnight. These hours can be reduced somewhat on weekends after the games without too much harm. Too much sleep can often be more harmful than not enough.

Under ordinary conditions of everyday living, elimination of body wastes becomes habitual. When traveling, however, conditions become different and care must be taken to keep elimination habits in regular operation. Additional fruit or fruit juices will sometimes help this condition when traveling. If these fail, laxatives should be used to help the players so their body will not become sluggish as the result of poor elimination.

Along with these practices, a boy should always have a good physical examination before the season starts. This will help to protect you and the boy. A youngster should never participate if he is ill, or immediately after recovering from an illness, unless he has a doctor check his condition. Winning should never be placed above the welfare of a boy's health. Many times a boy will tell you he is ready when he is a picture of bad health.

It is the responsibility of the coach to prepare his team mentally and physically for the game. The athlete has to cooperate with the coach to achieve this. Through good harmony and an understanding of what is necessary to win, these goals are reached with less effort. No other faculty member has to pass public scrutiny as often as the coach. Every time your team plays, you are examined by a very critical public. If your team wins, some of the examiners will give you a passing grade, while others will question you. If your team loses, you fail the examination in all respects, regardless of conditions.

This assignment you accept as a coach has many thrills and many headaches. Your leadership, counsel, guidance, and instruction develops many fine men. This development has to be achieved through proper organization, example, and leadership. If you can excel in these qualities, you may remain on the payroll even after a losing season. You will build the confidence of your players by insisting on important things. Morale, good conditioning, and fair treatment of all will help to retain their confidence. Once their confidence in you is lost, then you are lost and your coaching days are numbered. Be strong for all the things you believe in and be fair and patient. If you can display these virtues, with excellent teaching methods, your teams will win more than their share of games and you will be respected in your school and community.

• 6 •

Stressing Related Drills and Lead-Up Games

- -

Drills related to developing basketball skills can be utilized in early season practices with great benefits. Various games will develop similar skills in basketball that can be used to increase efficiency in play. Wise use of drills and lead-up games will increase the fun of learning skills which otherwise would be monotonous and ineffective. It is the responsibility of the coach to get the most from his material through proper organization, good morale, understanding, and hard work. Although these points must be considered, you must understand that the game of basketball was originated to bring joy in playing and pleasure in watching. Through proper preparation and training, confidence to achieve can be instilled in boys by different methods. When this confidence exists, young men can face the challenge of competition with a feeling of preparedness. They can also adjust to meet the complete surprise strategy that opponents use to create bewilderment.

The following related exercises as drills contribute much to the conditioning and developing of skills for a basketball squad:

1. Rope jumping.
2. Medicine ball drills.
3. Running and agility development.
4. Use of weights.

Rope Jumping

Many boys improve rapidly and efficiently in these related drills. In early practice sessions, usually the first three weeks of practice, have each boy spend considerable time with the jumping rope. Do not concern yourself with the development of fancy routines in jumping the rope. Instead, work toward having your players develop timing, rhythm, coordination, and leg development. Through leg conditioning, the boy is assured somewhat against injury to the ankle or knee.

Have your squad members spend approximately three minutes daily jumping the rope in this early practice. As the season progresses, insist that all your big men use the drill daily. The smaller men may be excused from rope jumping after three weeks unless they need special help. The bigger man needs a continuation of rope jumping to help his agility and coordination as well as his conditioning. Since the larger boy's growth is more rapid than the average boy, his coordination is not as advanced and he needs this extra activity as he matures. The large boy loses more efficiency in skills during a few days of inactivity than the smaller boy.

The responsibility of having ropes available during the early season for the entire group should be assigned to your team manager. After this period is ended, assign a rope to each one of your big men and make him responsible for this activity. In spite of the boys' enthusiasm and interest, check daily to make sure they do this exercise. Time spent on rope jumping will contribute much to the success of your team.

There are differences of opinion concerning the value of team calisthenic drills including exercises to strengthen and develop the fingers, wrists, hands and other parts of the arm and shoulder. Many coaches use calisthenics to achieve these results, and they have faith in the drills as a means for developing the arm and shoulder areas.

Medicine Balls

For best results, develop these body areas while practicing the fundamentals of basketball. The use of medicine balls in passing drills will lead to the physical development as well as contribute to better execution of these same skills needed in your offense. Follow the same procedure you apply with the jumping ropes by using the medicine balls during the first three weeks of practice. Never hesitate, however, to use medicine balls during the season if members of the team need this type of activity.

Use the medicine ball comparable in size to the basketball and weighing approximately six pounds. Players often comment in early season about how advantageous it would be to play the first game of the season with a medicine ball instead of the regulation basketball. One thing would certainly exist if this were done: there would be no excessive dribbling.

Passing drills with the medicine ball will develop passing skills. Boys have a great deal of fun using the medicine ball in fast passing drills and follow the heavier ball with the basketball in the same drills. The difference in the weight of the two balls results in very fast passing by a team member. You must always beware of monotony entering into drills because of its effect on the learning process. Make it a point to vary drills and have some competition to allow for fun during the everyday performance in these drills. Always be concerned with the proper conditioning of the body, which has to be in excellent condition to play present-day basketball. Boys should be able to play 32 or 40 minutes as the game requires or they should not be on the floor.

Running and Agility Drills

With all the running necessary in today's game, stress the importance of the proper care of the feet. Obtain the best shoes and the best equipment for your team. Careful conditioning of the feet and legs results in the least possible chance of injury. Have your boys do a lot of straight running to begin the season. Running distances and relays contributes to leg conditioning. After the feet are conditioned by distance running and relays, and hardened somewhat by specially prepared liquids, practice angle cuts, starts and stops, change of direction and other maneuvers. You will have less trouble with blisters and other foot conditions if proper care is taken to condition the feet properly through running. Nothing is more bothersome than sore feet or tired aching legs. Do not have that condition affect the performance or the morale of your squad.

Use of Weights

The late Bucky O'Connor and his colleagues in the Physical Education Department at the University of Iowa introduced the use of weights to develop skills for basketball. The object of their training program was strengthening of wrists and improving jumping ability through the use of weights. Wrist curls with the forearm resting on a hurdle helped hand and wrist development. The use of light barbells in various movements proved helpful in developing leg muscles used in jumping. With the light barbell placed on the shoulders at the back of the neck, the toes are placed on a piece of wood on the floor 2 inches high. The player then raises his body on the toes, bringing the heels two or more inches off the floor. The same weight barbell placed in the same postion was used, starting with an upright walk, going down to a squat walk, and returning to the upright position.

Evidence released on the use of these weights showed jumping ability was increased from 3 to 6 inches. Care must be taken however, not to overdo these drills or use heavy weights which might do more harm than good. These drills are recommended in early season and should not exceed 10 minutes a day.

Lead-Up Games

Lead-up games such as volley ball, handball, and tennis, together with some shadow boxing, will contribute to many skills employed in basketball. The diversion of play will also contribute to the joy and satisfaction of your team. Stress the importance of participation in these lead-up games for development and variety of play. These related activities can lead to increased proficiency in the game. Certainly participation in these games will offer opportunities such as association with other people, learning of new skills, and a variation of activity.

Volley ball play will add to a boy's ability to gain position while a ball is in flight, in addition to increasing his tipping ability. Setting the ball up for a spiking situation involves finger-tip control with one and two hands similar to the skills necessary in basketball for effective tipping. Timing the jump with the ball will also be helped.

In handball the ability to react quickly and gain position to play the ball develops quicker reflexes and makes for better footwork and recovery. Usually the better basketball players make the best handball players. Tennis offers the same opportunities as handball. The ability to maneuver quickly to play various tennis shots will add to the abilities of the basketeer.

Shadow boxing will help to develop the footwork needed to play the defensive game. Bigger men gain more development in these lead-up games than smaller men. The benefits of participation for both, however, will be beneficial to all and should increase respective skills as they are applied to basketball.

Spring Sports

Encourage your squad to participate in baseball or track after your season is completed. Your boys will be better basketball players because of these new experiences and development. If they do not have the abilities necessary to participate in the spring sports, insist on their working out to improve their play and to stay in physical condition. Track participation will add a great deal to skills in basketball. Starting speed can be improved if a boy is a sprinter. Jumping ability may be increased in the high jump. The hurdles improve speed and timing. Baseball will help speed and reaction time. Catching skills are also improved through participation in this spring sport.

With no organized practice allowed in the spring, squad members not participating in other sports have to organize and workout on their own. You should encourage them to improve their weaknesses and by so doing improve their abilities and value to the team. The dedicated player will work hard to improve his skills. You may have to check him to make sure he does not overwork. The lazy player, with ability, will have to be encouraged to participate in some practice out of season. Greatness in play is not developed only during the season. The great player is one who works the year round to improve his play.

Related drills and participation in lead-up games will contribute much to the success of your teams. There are many different ways of accomplishing the same results. All ideas have many arguments pro and con. Improvement in play, regardless of how it is developed, will be worth while in any sport activity.

• 7 •

Increasing the Team's Shooting Accuracy

Is the ability to shoot well more important than the ability to pass
well? What offensive technique is the most important?

Since basketball is a game of skills blended into a working unit,
speculation on which skills are most vital is inconsequential. The
team that passes and handles the ball expertly but lacks accurate
shooters is considerably handicapped. Contrariwise, the best
shooters in the game won't score often enough to win games unless
the team is adept at controlling the ball long enough to get good
shots.

Despite the fact that good shooting and good ball handling
go hand in hand, the ability to shoot will compensate for other
weaknesses in the offensive game. Strive to make each man on
your team a dependable, accurate shooter. If you have even
one weak shooter, your opponents will capitalize on this short-
coming. They will let this man play unguarded in close areas
in order to allow two men to defense a better shooter. Defensive
strategy such as this is quite common against poor shooters. Your
offensive play will suffer when all of your men aren't able to
shoot well enough to force the defense to play them all the way.

GREAT SHOOTERS—BORN OR MADE?

There is no doubt that great shooters possess inherent abilities that make great shooting skill possible. In addition to this inherent ability, however, the player must master proper fundamentals, generally referred to as good form, or he may not be effective.

In your teaching procedure always stress orthodox principles necessary to shoot effectively. Some boy may use an unorthodox form in shooting and make a better percentage of shots than those shooting according to "Hoyle." Many boys with the inherent shooting touch could be better shooters through proper instruction. This instruction should be given the boys early in their careers when they are learning the game. Youngsters playing in backyards learn to shoot effectively using improper form. If these boys can get the job done for you by shooting accurately and consistently, some thought should be given the problem before attempting to change them. Sometimes a change in form will upset their pattern and cause then to miss shots. In most cases, however, proper teaching will make them better shooters. Proper instruction, along with God's gift of ability to the boy, should result in better shooting performance. Conversely, you may not want to change a players shooting form if he operates successfully in an unorthodox manner; two points are two points.

TWO POINTS A MINUTE—WEAK DEFENSE OR STRONG OFFENSE?

When teaching the various shooting techniques, stress balance, concentration, release, follow through, arch, and recovery. Most present-day team candidates are much better shooters than was usual in previous years. Such factors as better coaching, earlier beginning practice, and new types of shots are responsible for this. Many years ago newspaper men and spectators were praising teams for their point-a-minute performance. Nowadays most teams are averaging two points or more over the forty-minute game period. This evidence alone is sufficient proof that some improvement along the way has made this greater point production possible.

Many critics contend the high scores exist because coaches are not teaching defense in the present-day game. Actually the average coach is spending more time on defensive preparation than ever before. He has no other alternative, for such shots as the hook shot and jump shot, when executed correctly, certainly make the defensive job tougher than before these two shots were used. The defense must be more sound and more time must be spent in teaching defense to at least slow the offensive pace.

PRACTICE SITUATIONS VERSUS GAME SITUATIONS

The proper use of a certain type shot, as well as the time the shot should be taken, is of great importance. Considerable time spent in practicing various shots is necessary if the player is to improve his shooting percentage. Game conditions should be emphasized and practiced to put some "pressure" on the shooter. It is always easy to shoot unmolested in practice. In a game or scrimmage, when the opposition is constantly harassing and pressing, the shooting situation suddenly becomes different. Most shooting drills should be practiced with an opponent giving the boys some opposition. In this action, the shooter is able to practice getting his shot away quicker and to shoot the ball in a manner that will lessen the chance of the opponent blocking it. The defense can help the shooter by merely raising the hand to force the ball to a necessary arch. It will also provide an opportunity to disregard the hand of the opponent and concentrate on the basket.

To begin your shooting instruction, start with the easiest shot in basketball, the lay-up shot, sometimes referred to as the set-up. Even though the lay-up is the simplest shot in the game, many times it is missed when the player gets the opportunity.

THE LAY-UP SHOT

Require a high accuracy or percentage on the lay-up shot. Your team will not get many of these shots if the defense plays a zone defense or fills the middle area in front of the basket. Establish a goal of at least 90 per cent accuracy (if possible 100 per cent) with the lay-up shot. This shot is often missed because it appears too easy to make. Explanation of the various important points of good lay-up shooting should include the following:

1. Holding the ball properly.
2. Protection of the ball.
3. The target.
4. Take-off foot and position.
5. The follow through.
6. The recovery after the shot.

Your team should practice this shot, with its variations, from all the possible angles of approach the opponents will force you to take. The appropriate use of the hands and the take-off foot must be checked thoroughly to obtain proper results. The position of the take-off will vary with a boy's height. Proper jumping and maximum height of the jump will help increase the accuracy.

The Ball

Instruction can begin by teaching players to hold the ball properly for accurate release. Holding the ball on the fingertips with no part of it touching the heel of the hand will result in a better touch. The opposite hand plays an important part in the shot as a balance and partial guide, to help get the ball to the necessary height before its release. The opposite forearm and elbow of the shooting side will give some protection to keep the ball from being knocked loose. When attempting the lay-up shot, the take-off foot should be opposite the shooting hand. In other words, if the shot is made with the right hand the take-off should be from the left foot and vice-versa. In this action, greater height can be reached and better adjustment can be made. Accuracy will also improve. Youngsters should strive to get a thrill in jumping high and releasing the ball off the bankboard with a feather touch.

The Eyes

The eyes should be focused upon the spot on the bankboard that will be used to bank the ball into the basket. Sometimes a boy will focus his vision on the basket when attempting the lay-up. Concentration of vision on the basket instead of on the spot on the bankboard will cause shots to be unsuccessful. At the height of the jump your player should push the ball off the guiding hand and follow through with the force necessary to complete the shot.

The Hand

At the time the ball is released the palm of the shooting hand should face the bankboard as the arm is extended. This release will enable your player to get more height for the ball. Proper mechanics will also allow the player to increase or lessen the force placed on the ball. The lay-up shot made by using the hand with the palm up and facing the ceiling will not enable the greatest height. Using this form also requires an improper release of the ball as the force is brought about by pulling away from the ball or flipping it with a shovel action. Accuracy is reduced in this case as it is harder to control the release and flight of the ball.

The Jump

You should concern yourself with the player's jumping technique when shooting the lay-up. As the boy drives in for this shot, he must employ proper timing to get the correct foot in place for the effective takeoff. A shooter can be in trouble if he takes off too soon or too late. A slowing down action to gather himself for the jump is necessary to obtain maximum spring off the legs to get up in the air. Many boys shoot incorrectly and often miss shots because they broad jump and flip the ball toward the basket as they go by. Broad jumping and successful lay-up shooting do not complement each other. The high jump pays greater dividends to gain points. Certain key marks on the floor can be used to help the boy adjust his shot. The take-off spot will vary, depending on the height and speed of the boy. On an angle approach from the side, the free-throw lane marks will serve as a good key for the take-off spot. On the front approach, two short steps beyond the free throw line will be a desirable key for the take-off.

The Recovery

In recovering after the shot, players should not land too far outside the end line. This spot of alighting will indicate the difference between high jumping and broad jumping. Softness of the shot is necessary. Always remind the "bankboard testers" (who bank the ball so hard it rebounds to the free throw line) that the bankboard was tested at the factory and needs no further testing. Remind these shooters to "ooze" the ball off the board or "put feathers on the ball." Proper recovery will result in being able to act quickly if the basket is made or missed. Recovering on defense if the basket is made or gaining position for a possible rebound if the basket is missed, is the desirable action.

The Opposite as Well as the Natural Way

In order to be a constant threat to the opponents, a player should be able to use both hands effectively around the basket. When a boy is unable to use both hands, the defense will capitalize on this weakness. Forcing the boy to the side on which he is incapable will cause him to shoot with the hand he doesn't have confidence in. If he can go both ways and shoot well the defense will not be able to overplay your player and force his weakness. Inasmuch as most boys are right handed, considerable time must be spent in developing the left hand for shooting. The same form should be used with either hand considering, of course, the take-off foot being opposite the shooting hand.

When considerable trouble in adjusting to the shots is encountered, break the shot down into its simplest fundamentals. Dribbling and ball handling will help develop the left hand. Placing the boy one step from the take-off spot will help the adjustment to the left hand shot. One step with the right foot and the take-off using the left hand is a fundamental drill to teach habit and confidence. Dribbling in to attempt the shot will help young players adjust. Breaking in fast and receiving a pass for the lay-up is also a good drill for teaching the use of the opposite hand. The use of the bankboard will increase accuracy and create proper form. Sometimes a shooter will get in the air and try to decide whether to bank the shot or shoot over the basket rim. This hesitation will result in a missed shot in a majority of attempts.

The Various Lay-Up Approaches

All angles of approach should be practiced as the defense will force you to use these angles. When practicing the lay-up shot have your boys come in from the right side using the right hand. The left side approach should be used with the left hand shot. Coming in from the same angle, players should cross in front of the basket for the lay-back shot with a pivot effected on the inside foot to get proper balance and recovery for rebounding. Driving from the corners along the baseline will require practice. To make this shot a player needs to drive under the basket and lay the ball back with the lead hand. The 4-foot space between the endline and the bankboard has made this shot an effective one.

The defense, trying to force the player out, has a tendency to relax momentarily on the false assumption that the possible shooter is out of position to make the shot. This offers an opportunity to "sneak" the ball up on a bank shot. Coming in from the left side of the basket results in the shot being attempted with the right hand. The left hand is used on the attempt from the right side of the basket. Approaching the basket from the front necessitates a direction to either side of the basket for the best shot.

Dunk If Possible

If your boys can jump well enough, encourage them to "dunk" the ball. Having a few boys on the team who can dunk the ball serves as a stimulus to the smaller boys. This constant challenge will help the jumping abilities of your squad. Occasionally on a front approach the defense will force your player to the side of the basket. A push shot with a pivot off the inside leg is a good shot from this angle. A hook shot on the run from this angle is impossible to stop.

Drills for the various approaches should point out the need for angle cuts toward the basket. Angle cuts are more effective in outmaneuvering the defense. At the same time practice of this technique will help improve team effort for better screening. A combination of the two actions presented with shooting drills will help to increase fundamental execution.

Angles Used to Practice the Lay-Up Shot

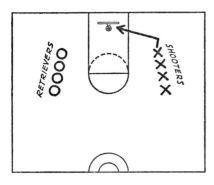

Fig. 157. Right side approach for right-hand lay up.

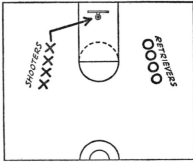

Fig. 158. Left side approach for left-hand lay up.

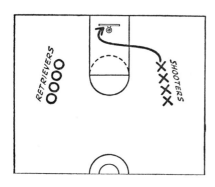

Fig. 159. Cross over for left-hand lay back.

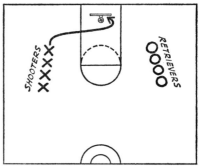

Fig. 160. Cross over for right-hand lay back.

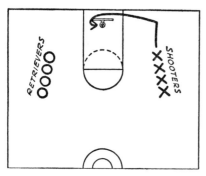 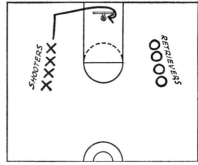

Fig. 161. Base line drive with left-hand bank shot.

Fig. 162. Base line drive with right-hand bank shot.

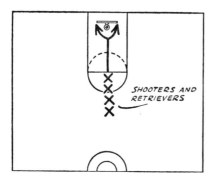 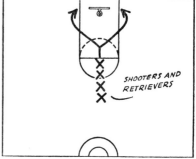

Fig. 163. Straight approach with veering to either side for lay up with right or left hand.

Fig. 164. Force out shot with pivot action toward basket off take-off foot on inside. Hook shot also from this angle if possible.

THE ONE-HAND SHOT

The introduction of the one-hand shot to basketball was readily accepted and contributed a great deal to the game. The theory of the one-hand shot was feasible and readily accepted. Arguments favored this shot over the two-handed shot because there was only one pressure on the ball. In the two-handed shot unequal force caused the ball to veer in direction. The one-hand push shot had no chance for this unequal pressure and was accepted as a better shot. The one-hand shot can be used from a set position and while on the move. In most cases, the two-hand shot was only effective as a set shot. You should teach all your boys the proper fundamentals of the one-hand shot for better shooting results.

As in any teaching process, many details must be considered and taught to make the skill better. The most important points in teaching one-hand shots are:

1. Good balance.
2. Concentration.
3. Relaxation.
4. Proper release of ball.
5. Adequate height and arch.
6. Good follow through.

The legs and body must be coordinated with the action of the arm, wrist, hands and fingers. Additional force from greater distance can be acquired with the feet and legs when the hands and arms are not sufficient.

Proper Balance

Inasmuch as most players like to use the one-hand shot, the teaching and learning process is easier and quicker than other shots. The first essential to consider in teaching this shot is the proper balance of the body. The feet should be spread comfortably with the same foot forward as the hand used in shooting. If the shooter is right handed, the right foot should precede the left foot in the stance and vice versa for the left-handed shooter. The other foot should be approximately 14 to 18 inches from the lead foot and to the side. The toe of the rear foot should be even with the long arch of the lead foot to insure good balance. The distance between the two feet of the shooter will vary according to the height of the individual. The taller the boy, the greater distance between foot spread will be required for good balance.

The knees should be slightly bent straight forward with most of the weight of the body on the balls of the feet. The back should be rigid with a slight lean forward from the hips. The head must be erect with the eyes focusing on the front rim of the basket. The point of focus is often argued. Some coaches indicate the focus of the eyes should be on the back rim of the basket. From the floor position the front rim is easier to see and can be detected quicker. After much practice, however, the vision probably centers on the whole basket area and the ball is shot without too much concentration on either the front or back rim.

Holding the Ball

When placing the shooting hand on the ball, the fingers should be spread comfortably over the ball. The hand should be across the seams of the ball and not parallel to them in the early process of teaching the shot. This teaching factor is not too important as the boy progresses with his shooting for he may not have time to adjust the ball this way in a game. He must be able to catch the ball and shoot quickly without the thought of adjustment and position of the ball. During the primary phase of teaching, the placing of the ball as mentioned gives the boy a better feeling of the balance of the ball. To delay action in a game to get proper positioning of the ball can result in the defense blocking the shot.

Both hands should be used in the one-hand shot. The opposite hand is used to support the ball. The force of the shooting hand pushes the ball off its resting place. The resting hand also helps to guide the ball. The ball should be held at shoulder height and off to one side of the face in order not to block the vision of the shooter. When the ball is held in front of the face there is a temporary blocking of vision as the ball is brought up for the release. From the position off the shoulder, the ball can be shot, passed or used with a fake and drive.

The Release

When the shot is started, the ball should remain at shoulder level. As the knees are slightly bent forward the ball will drop naturally with the body. Sometimes boys will drop the ball by bending the wrists to get more force in the shot. This action drops the ball and hands sometimes as much as 12 inches. You should check this action as it slows the shot sufficiently to allow the defense to move in closer to your player. The shot must still be brought up for release and the additional force needed should come from the legs. As the shooting and resting arm are extended, the ball can be brought up close to the side of the face for a better arch and follow through. The elbow should be close to the side of the body and not up and out.

When the ball is released, there should be a slight spin of the ball toward the shooter. A dead ball or one that floats is released from the heel of the hand. Such a release does not provide the touch necessary for good shooting. The softer the spin, the softer the touch of the ball. The soft shot will help the ball to rest on the rim sometimes and drop through even though the shot is not too accurate. The hard spin will carom the ball off the board or basket much faster.

The Follow-Through and Proper Arch

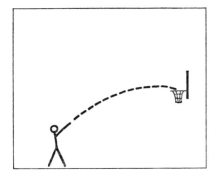 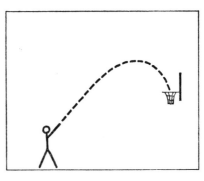

Fig. 165. Straight arch. Fig. 166. Medium arch.

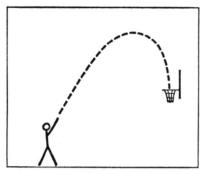

Fig. 167. Roof duster arch.

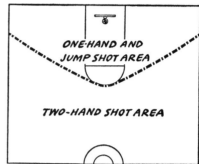

Fig. 168. Shooting areas.

As the ball is released off the fingers and not the palm or heel of the hand, the arch of the shot should be sufficient to be well above the basket. Three types of arches used in shooting are:

1. The straight arch.
2. The medium arch.
3. The exaggerated arch.

The straight arch is directed almost straight toward the rim of the basket. If the shot is made, it must hit the back rim perfectly to force the ball through the basket. The medium arch is shot at a height of 6 to 8 feet above the basket with the necessary distance in front of the basket to allow the ball to drop in at the basket area. The "roof duster" arch is the exaggerated type which is seldom used. This arch is used when the ball is shot extremely high. The ball may be shot as high as 15 or 20 feet above the basket when this form is used. The medium arch provides the best chance for the ball to go through the basket. A softer shot is made possible with the medium arch. The flight of the ball in the three arches can be shown by drawing and demonstration. Proper demonstration will impress your players.

To get the proper follow-through on the shot, the arm must be fully extended. As the ball is released the wrist should break forward and the palm of the hand will face the floor. Many boys flip the hand and arm backward as the ball is released. This action does not allow good follow-through causing the shot to be short and in most cases hitting the front rim of the basket. The pattern may be comparable to a hitter in baseball or a golfer stopping his swing the instant the ball is hit. There is no follow-through motion on the swing, hence power and distance are lacking.

Great Hands—Great Shooters

A great one-handed shooter will in most cases, possess great and supple hands and wrists. With these two qualities, a boy can get sufficient force for the necessary distance. If the boy does not possess good hands and wrists he will have to get some force from his body and legs. A slight jump off the floor will help this force and add rhythm to the shot. Some boys are born with great hands, others need help to develop better hands. It becomes your job to help each type of boy. The one with great hands can be helped with proper shooting instructions. The boy with poor hands will need ball handling and passing drills to develop good hands.

The Moving One-Hand Shot

The one-hand shot may be used as a set shot which has been explained, or it may be used on the move, if the defense is not too close to the shooter. This shot has the same principles of execution as the set shot, with the exception that a step is taken with the opposite foot. As this step is taken with the opposite foot the other foot is brought up with the bending of the knee to get good balance with the shot. The shot is started and released the same as the one-hand set shot. It is comparable to the lay-up shot with the distance necessary for the flight of the ball being greater. Both of these shots can be used with a screen or a fake to make the defense release. Against zone defenses, these shots can be used well after the passing of the ball has moved the defense to give time for the shot.

THE JUMP SHOT

The jump shot, along with the hook shot, is very difficult to defense in modern day basketball. These two shots when managed correctly, are almost impossible to stop. The universal acceptance and use of these two shots has contributed to the larger scores in the game today. Defenses are working overtime to attempt ways and means of stopping these two shots.

Jump-Shot Situations

There are two ideal situations for use of the jump shot if the factors of equal height and abilities exist between two opponents:

1. Off a dribble when the defense is retreating and has the way blocked for continued advancement.
2. When a player comes off a screen and can shoot before the defense makes the adjustment.

A jump shot, because of the mechanics involved in its execution, cannot be too effective outside a 20-foot radius. If it is effective beyond this distance the shooter needs strong wrists and fingers. Consequently, you should prescribe a certain radius for your players.

The Front Approach

The jump shot has many principles identical to that of the one-hand set shot. The player using this shot can get better height with balance when the takeoff force comes from both feet. The shot should begin at shoulder level with the opposite hand serving as a ball rest and partial guide. Your player should jump as high as possible with legs straight and slightly spread for good recovery. Using this leg position the boy may be jostled and still keep his balance. The legs should never be bent sharply under the body since this position will affect the balance and the recovery of the shooter.

As the extension of the shooting arm occurs on the jump, the ball should be released off the finger tips at the extreme height of the jump. The ball should never be released while going up, or while coming down. The timing of the release of the ball at the apex of the jump is very important. Without this timing the shot is not coordinated with rhythmic movement of the body. In this event the force has to come mainly from the wrists and fingers and in most cases it is not sufficient. When a player approaches the basket from the front, he needs to place both feet on the floor before he can jump properly and shoot. The placing of both feet allows more force and creates better balance than when the jump is attempted off one foot. The release, the arch and the follow-through should be the same as the one-hand shot. Recovery on both feet gives your player a better chance to follow the shot and rebound.

The Side Approach

When a boy moves from the sideline in or from the center of the floor out, the footwork used in the jump shot changes. While attempting this maneuver, have your player place the lead foot on the floor with more force than the follow-up foot. This step is necessary to stop body momentum from continuing, naturally resulting in a direction of the ball in line with his momentum. As the lead foot is placed hard on the floor, the other foot must be brought into place causing the force of the jump to initiate off both feet. If the body is kept straight, the shooter can jump higher and at the same time retain better body balance to release the ball.

Basketball has many great jump shooters today. To defense them correctly is almost an impossibility. Sometimes players use a fall-away technique with the jump shot making the shot more effective and harder to stop. Other forms used in making the jump shot have been successful. In 1957 we had a player named Steinke, who used a jack-knife action of the body with his jump shot. He was a very good shooter because he possessed fine hands and strong wrists. His form was contrary to the orthodox way of shooting, but the boy still hit the shot with a good percentage. Incidentally, we did not try to force him to shoot orthodox after he convinced us he could make baskets with his particular style.

The Hook and Post Variety

The hook shot, when used correctly, is practically impossible to stop. This shot accompanied by the jump shot really makes the task of defensing more complicated. In general play, there are two types of hook shots being employed today. One is the close-in hook using the bankboard for the target. The other type is the longer hook aimed directly at the basket and used considerably farther from the basket. This latter type has become famous because of its use by Coach Tippy Dye at Washington. Such names as Houbregs, Smart, Boin and others are prominent because of the success they have had with this sensational hook shot. These men have served as good examples for prospective players to imitate. Such examples result in earlier periods of practice and more effort to duplicate the action of outstanding players.

Due to the effectiveness of the hook shot and inability to stop it, most defenses now set up to prevent the post man from getting the ball. By playing a defensive man in front or on the side of the post man the defense has been able to contest the pass in. As the post man is being played in this manner it is necessary that defensive men on the side and in front drop off their men to attempt double teaming. Many teams now use the small man in the post position. With his abilities to maneuver and shoot, good results are secured. This offensive move with the small man in, however, will weaken the board power of his team. Regardless of the strategy used, the post man must have a good supporting cast from the outside to keep the defense open.

Side Feed or Front Feed?

Passing to the post man from the side of the floor is conceded to be better than feeding him from the front. The side feed became more effective than the front feed when the free throw lane was widened. Many teams still use the front feed, however, with excellent results. Regardless of the best passing area, the post man must be able to maneuver well to evade the defense. If he is unable to get free, he can never receive the pass. To be free to receive the pass the post man must be able to fake well, change direction, and, as a last resort, set a high post position at the free-throw line. Clear outs and players going through for screening purposes are being used with good results in getting the ball inside. To get more space to maneuver, the post man in most offenses will set up opposite the ball. He is then in a better position to maneuver and avoid the congestion of the free-throw area.

Teaching the Hook Shot

When teaching the hook shot, break it down into the details of the simplest form. Your post man should be able to hook well with either hand. This desire places a lot of responsibility on the boy and requires many hours of work and diligent practice. If you do not have the boy who can master this, your offensive punch will be decreased considerably. Most college coaches seek the high school graduate who can hook well with either hand. Their teaching job is simplified and the offense is more potent when this boy is added to the squad. As a high school coach, your job of teaching a boy becomes more painstaking and certainly more time consuming.

Must Be Able to Fake Too!

Instruction in post play should begin by emphasizing the movements necessary to get free to receive the pass. Angle direction with fakes and change-ups will help to achieve this goal. The post man must always move to meet the ball. He may use a shuffle step out or set a high post in addition to meeting the ball. After receiving the ball, your post man should be taught to use head and shoulder fakes opposite the side of the proposed hook shot. This faking serves a purpose in keeping the defense slightly loose and making him hesitate momentarily. A step fake should not be used with the head and shoulder fake as it establishes the pivot foot and forces the direction one way. The post man has a different problem than the other four players in that his back is to the basket in his operations.

When the head and shoulder fake is made the ball should be held in the midsection for protective reasons. The eyes should be focused over the faking shoulder to determine any movement of the defense. If the defensive man goes for the fake or is playing too close, your post player should be able to wheel and drive for the basket. Sometimes your pivot player will be able to hook the leg of his opponent as he wheels creating good position and a step advantage on the defense. In the event the defense plays in front or on the side of your post man and the latter has space to maneuver, he can block out with his body and take a lob pass over and in front of the basket. When the defensive man loosens on the head and shoulder fake the hook shot opportunity is available.

After the head and shoulder fake is made, teach your hook shooters to step slightly toward the basket with the lead foot. There must be no step with the fake or your player will violate when he executes the steps necessary for the shot. As the lead step is made, the ball should be brought up with both hands and a pivot made off the lead foot. The eyes at this stage must be looking over the inside shoulder and focusing on the spot on the board to use a bank shot or at the basket directly. The opposite elbow of the shooting arm is raised with the forearm and the hand for control of the ball and to protect the ball from the defense. The ball is released as the shooting arm is extended with a roll off the finger tips and not the palm. The ball should never be wrist flipped while making the shot. The flip will cause less accuracy and a lower arch. The arch of the ball should be fairly high so the shot is harder to block and the ball arrives at the basket with an easy touch. In the release and follow-through of the shot, the upper part of the shooting arm should touch the ear on that side for a straighter flight and better body balance. To shoot with the upper part of the arm back of the head results in poor shooting balance and tightens the muscles. Tension results and accuracy is decreased. To bring the upper arm in front of the head results in a swing shot and gives the defense more of an opportunity to stop the shot.

The Recovery

As a slight jump is made off the pivot foot the ball should be released off the finger tips much like the action in a hook pass. You can then instruct your post man to recover by alighting with both feet facing the basket with the body in a position to rebound. Some players have a habit of falling away from the basket after the release of the ball permitting the opponent all the advantage on the board. You must attempt to get the second shot if the first one is missed and contest hard for that chance. After proper recovery is made, stress movement toward the basket to fight for the rebound. The mechanics of the shot as described also permit better balance, more accurate release of the ball and conform with good shooting procedure.

THE POP SHOT

Teaching the details of the pop shot can easily follow instructions of the hook shot as the movement in both shots is exactly alike to a certain stage. The natural shooting hand should be used with this shot as the shot is used from a distance which makes the opposite hand less productive. This distance would be comparable to the close hooking areas. The hook shot details precede the pop shot in order to cause the defense to hesitate while determining which shot will be used. The head and shoulder fake must be made with the lead step taken as if to hook. The eyes are again focused over the shoulder spotting the bankboard area.

As the mechanics of the shot proceed this far the shooter can use the step out with the lead foot as a pivot and turn to the side favoring the shooting hand. A jump is made off the pivot foot and with a slight turn of the body inside, the quick shot is attempted. With the possibility of either shot being made off the maneuver, the defense cannot commit quickly which allows some freedom in the shot. If the defensive man is expecting the hook and steps to match your post man's lead step, the pop shot is open. The defensive man may expect the pop shot and, by hesitating, let your post man have more freedom and time to attempt the hook shot.

The Step-Out Shot

The step-out shot is similar to the pop shot with the only changes being the direction of the lead step and the recovery. In the hook and pop shot details, the lead step is taken with a slight gain of distance toward the basket. In the step-out shot, the lead step is made away from the basket to gain distance on the defensive man. The pivot, turn and jump movement is made off the lead foot with a fall-away motion of the body away from the basket. This shot must be attempted in the close hooking region to secure best results. The principles of orthodox shooting are violated in that the body moves away from the shot. Again, strong wrists and fingers must be able to compensate for the lack of force from the body. The recovery position will not be conducive to good rebounding.

Fake and Wheel

Every post man should be able to fake and wheel or reverse pivot and drive for the basket. This maneuver is made possible by the defense over committing on a fake and opening the lane to drive. The post man must be able to recognize the defensive mistake quickly and react to take advantage of it. As a result, much time must be spent in drill for recognition purposes. Have your post men work together in early daily practice to help with these details. One man should be faking, maneuvering and shooting with another post man defensing him. The feeder may be your outside man or another post man if you have three. As the players work on this drill, all the movements and shots may be practiced as the defense allows them. Occasionally have your defensive man make an obvious mistake to see if the offensive man is thinking and reacting properly to the movement.

The Small Man Can Hook Too!

Sometimes you can use small players in the post area if they can hook and maneuver well. If some of the team can hook well on certain occasions, you should capitalize on this ability. We had a small boy named Tebbs, who at 5'9" made the Little All-American team for two years. He could execute a hook shot very well from the right side of the basket and out 10 to 12 feet. He scored many points with this shot as he came off a screen and forced the defense to switch with him. The fans were always delighted to see this youngster hit the running hook shot over bigger men who switched off to stop the drive.

College teams have many forwards who are converted high school centers. If you have one of these boys who can hook well, your offense can be made more versatile. In 1951 Brigham Young University had a 6-foot boy named Minson who could operate well in the post position because of his excellent faking and speed. The boy had played this position in high school and knew the various maneuvers well. We used the boy in the post to capitalize on his abilities. Larger men were bewildered trying to defense him. In our quest for the N. I. T. Championship we alternated this boy in the post with Hutchins, our regular center. This change of position moved the opponent's big man off the board. By exchanging position of these men, Minson averaged 28 points per game over the three-night tournament. Our team won the championship and Minson won the most valuable player award for his excellent play inside and outside. Other teams have used little men in the post with good results.

THE FREE THROW

When the bonus free throw was allowed in basketball, the free-throw opportunity became more valuable. The opportunity to score two points on a foul compensated somewhat for loss of possession. Coaches wisely spent more time trying to increase free-throw accuracy and percentages. Thus, many drills and philosophies have been presented to achieve better free throwing. Several years ago, before the change in rules to the present free-throw rule, many games were won at the free-throw line by teams that were outscored from the field. At the same time, the number of fouls committed in a game was reduced, as it was too costly to foul when the opponents had consistent free throwers. The present rule still requires good free throwing if a team is to always present a threat and scoring balance with the offensive attack.

One Hand or Two Hand?

Pro and con arguments have been presented over a period of years concerning the best way to shoot free throws. Some critics contend that a player should shoot his free throws in the manner he shoots from the field. Candidates for higher degrees have written theses presenting the merits of the one-hand shot and the two-hand shot for free throws. The game has had great free throwers using one or the other shooting method with excellent results. You should have your players use the shot which they have the most confidence in and the one they can utilize more accurately. Inasmuch as most college prospects have a certain shot when they enroll, it may not be wise to change their style as long as they get results. Research and testing indicate that the two-handed underhand free throw shot produces better accuracy when fatigue enters the picture. On this basis, it might be well to introduce and teach this shot to youngsters learning the game because of that possibility. There have been many fine one-handed shooters, however, at the line, and improvement could not be too great in some instances. With an unmolested 15-foot shot a boy should make a good percentage with all factors being equal. Sometimes good shooters will be less accurate during the free throw attempt when nervous or mental factors are conducive to tenseness.

Considerable practice time should be planned to improve free-throw opportunities. While teaching and practicing the free throw, several things must be stressed. The following points need attention:

1. Relaxation.
2. Concentration.
3. Balance.
4. Arch of shot.
5. Target.
6. Follow-through.

Permit the players to use the shot they have confidence in if they are experienced players. Beginning players should be encouraged to specialize in shooting free throws one specific way. If a player has trouble with his free-throw percentage, do not hesitate to change his shot or his form immediately. Sometimes minor details need straightening out and the trouble is corrected instantly. In the event a boy changes his shot completely, immediate success is often experienced. This success will be followed by a plateau or a decrease in percentage which stimulates the boy to try another shot. If you allow him to change too often the boy becomes confused and he never corrects his problem. You must insist that a boy shoot his free throws one way or the other and stay with the shot until he improves and regains his confidence. If a boy can shoot at all, he should be able to make a good percentage of his free throws.

Practice Wisely

There are many drills used to practice free throws. You should vary free-throw drills somewhat to allow for competition and game conditions. Competition drills such as free-throw twenty-one, freeze-out and consecutive free throws will get away from routine practice. After strenuous running or maneuvering drills, free throws can be practiced during the rest period. The boys can regain their strength and at the same time practice the free-throw when some element of fatigue exists. You can take 10 minutes for this practice and have the boys get as many free throws as possible. This procedure can be repeated once or twice during the practice session. Sometimes during scrimmage have the boy fouled shoot three free throws regardless of the foul.

A competition game called free-throw twenty-one is interesting and profitable meanwhile creating some "pressure" on players free-throw shooting. In this game six boys can be used. They are divided three men to a team. Having three men on each side requires each man being numbered one through three . The number one man starts shooting free throws until he misses or makes three consecutive throws. When the ball is missed or the third free throw is made, the teams scrimmage at one basket until a field goal is made. In case the free throw is missed the ball may be tipped in or played for a field goal during the scrimmage. If the tip is made the boy making the tip-in basket gets the opportunity to go to the free throw line. The number one man on the opposing team takes his turn at free throws when the basket is made from scrimmage. This play is repeated with number two and three taking their respective turns on each team. When a foul is made, a jump ball occurs or an out-of-bounds happens, the next man in line shoots his free throws. This gives every boy a chance to make free throws somewhat under game conditions. The game is continued until 21 points are scored by a team. Free throws count one point and field goals count two. Your team will enjoy this competitive game and skills can be improved in free throwing under the simulated game conditions.

In all your free-throw practice, insist that a boy step back from the line and take a new position with each throw. This compares more with a game situation and reduces the chance of becoming fixed in a certain spot and making many shots without moving. The player has only two consecutive free throws at the most in the game, and stepping back will help him duplicate game conditions.

Freeze-out free-throw practice is very competitive and presents some of the "pressures" of game free throwing. Sometimes when a drill becomes monotonus, have the boys stop the drill and shoot free throws freeze-out style. This drill stimulates competition and places "pressure" on the boys to duplicate the shot of the man ahead of him. If the man ahead in the line makes his free throw, the man behind him has to make his free throw or he is disqualified from the game. If the man in front misses his shot, the player behind can make or miss his shot without a penalty. When the front man makes the shot, the player following has to do his best to remain in the game. Try to induce competition between the squad by classes such as sophomores, juniors and seniors. Competition by position namely, forwards, guards and centers will also make for good performance. The boys like the competition presented with this drill, and each boy does his best to avoid the humiliation of being eliminated from the contest.

You may also use a drill where a boy will attempt to make as many free throws as he can in consecutive numbers. This drill will stimulate the weak shooter to increase his free-throw attempts. The better free throwers get the practice in this activity with the poor shooters not receiving the practice. The chance to improve is always present, however, and it may stimulate the poor shooters to work harder to improve this skill.

Many coaches, pressed for sufficient practice time, will have their players shoot free throws during the lunch hour. Others will have their players shoot until they miss. These drills will not be suffcient and in most cases will not help the weaker free-throw shooter improve.

The free-throwing game is sometimes difficult to understand. What happens to a team when it can make 70 per cent or more of its free throws one night and have the percentage drop to 50 the next game? If you can answer the question and prescribe the proper remedy, you can make more money as an advisor and have fewer worries than a coach.

In 1957 our team was exceptional in its free-throwing achievements. The Skyline Championship was won by Brigham Young University largely because of accurate free throws. Several games

LAY UP SHOT. Take off from left foot. Right knee brought up to help with high jump. Take off distance is good. Protective left hand is in good position after release from ball. Right hand is in process of being turned up and out to get finger tip control and good release of ball.

ONE-HAND SET SHOT. Ball started up for release. Left hand is in good position to support ball until force is applied by right hand. Eyes are focused on basket. Slight turn of body is natural with right foot extended.

JUMP SHOT. This shot taken off dribble. Defense cannot recover to hinder shooter. Ball just released off left hand with force from right hand. Right arm and hand are in good follow-through position with arm extended and wrist broken down. Left hand is in good position. Legs and body are straight for good balance. Legs are in good position for recovery and rebound.

HOOK SHOT. Ball ready for release. Left forearm and hand are in good protective position. Eyes are focused on banking area. Take-off foot in slight pivot with opposite foot coming into place for rebound play.

TWO-HANDED CHEST PASS. Ball is held at chest level. Knees are slightly bent. Hands are placed comfortably on the ball. Elbows are close to body. Eyes are focused straight ahead with head erect. Body has good balance.

were won because opponents were outscored in free throws while our team was outscored from the field. The practice schedule for free throws called for the same drills as in previous years. What was the reason for this improvement? A tremendous team pride was developed and everyone tried hard to keep the percentages up. The team averaged 67 per cent with the top three free throwers shooting 84, 80 and 76 per cent respectively. In one game, the team made 18 free throws in 18 attempts during the second half. Another time the team made 16 of 17 free throws in the last four minutes when the opponents fouled in their attempt to gain possession of the ball.

In other games our free-throw percentage dropped to 50. Needless to say, the team lost these games. Just another good example of the variable existing in basketball. Pressure and tenseness certainly affect the accuracy of the free throw. To relieve this pressure get your boys to bounce the ball once or twice and take a deep breath before attempting the shot. Whether the breath is held during the shot depends on your thinking. The steps necessary to obtain maximum relaxation are needed to develop proper concentration and ultimate good free throwing. Inducing team pride in free throws can increase your overall percentage. As lay psychologists, coaches might capitalize on this opportunity. The team should be reminded often, however, of the goals in order to keep the object present in the mind of every player.

TIPPING

Considerable time should be spent in practice to improve tipping skills. Several easy baskets can be scored if your team knows how to put the ball back-up. Lead-up games previously mentioned will contribute to this art. Rope jumping and weights will also be helpful. Tipping covers will serve a good purpose to get repeated tipping practice.

Always have the tipping covers in place at the beginning of practice. These covers can be used on two baskets to get the desired work. Three minutes practice daily for all personnel during the first three weeks of practice will improve the technique. The taller men need to practice this drill each day during the season. The small men can drill once a week to keep in practice. Forming a triangle similar to the one used in the game offers the best opportunity. The ball keeps coming off the rim and a real workout is possible in the three minutes required. Jumping and timing skills are coordinated with the tipping practice.

When tipping the ball, your players should cushion the ball softly with the fingers. The ball can then be tipped with the fingers and wrists resulting in more accuracy. Do not allow your team members to fight the ball and slap it up hoping it will drop through. All of your personnel should know how to handle tipping chances as your little men are on the boards at certain times. Of course, smaller men should attempt to gain possession if possible and not try to tip with bigger men in the tipping zone.

Combine your offensive tipping practice with your defensive rebounding. With the competition more effectiveness will be achieved. Position for tipping must be obtained while the ball is in flight. If your boys cannot get position then it will be too late unless the opponents are weak on blocking out. That weakness is a rare thing nowadays. Tipping and rebounding drills will help the jumping ability of all your players. If your boys are good jumpers, strength on the boards will show tremendously. Jumping skill is very important in both offensive and defensive rebounding. Time spent on this in practice will pay dividends in the form of easy baskets— and the easy baskets count just as much as the hard ones.

THE TWO-HAND CHEST SHOT

The two-hand chest shot was very popular before the introduction of the one-hand shot. Although the shot is used today by a minority of players, some employ it with effective results. From an area of 25 feet or more from the basket, the two-hand chest shot is probably more accurate than the one-hand shot, due to the extra force available through the use of both hands. Basketball teams in the eastern part of the United States use this shot with more success than teams in other areas. Because they use this shot, the same teams probably excel in long-distance shooting. In the majority of sections, the youngsters favor the one-hand shot, and it becomes rather difficult to sell them on the merits of the two-hand shot. If you can convince your outside men to use the shot, you can increase your shooting threat beyond your opponent's usual zone of defense.

In teaching the two-hand chest shot, the same principles taught in the use of other shots should be stressed. These principles would include balance, concentration, holding the ball, follow-through, arch, and so on. The ball should be held the same as in the two-hand chest pass. If a boy can use the two-hand chest pass well, he should be able to use this shot with good results. The fingers should be spread comfortably on the side of the ball with the thumbs parallel. Some boys prefer placing the hands farther behind the ball, resulting in more of a push action to get the force. Holding the ball at face level, with eyes looking at the target over the top of the ball, allows for good concentration and still permits passing or faking from this position. The elbows need to be held close to the body and not up and out. When the elbows are raised, the thumbs are forced in too far on the ball and release must come from the thumbs entirely, thereby wasting arm action and affecting good follow-through. Bringing the ball up close to the face will get the necessary arch and make the shot more difficult to block. The arms need to be fully extended with the release of the ball off the thumbs and first fingers. Equal pressure by both hands in the release will insure a straight flight of the ball. Unequal pressure will cause the ball to veer in direction. As the ball is released, the palms of the hands should be facing the basket. This action insures proper follow-through necessary for accuracy in shooting.

The feet should be slightly spread to provide for good balance. There are two schools of thought regarding position of the feet. One advocates the feet being parallel, whereas the other school maintains one foot should be placed in advance of the other. For faking and driving purposes, having the feet parallel offers the best advantages. With the toes in line, the jab step in the drive can be made with either foot. When one foot is extended and the jab is made with the lead foot, the distance is greater, slowing down the second step needed for the advantage.

The body should be slightly bent forward at the hips. The bending knee action should be straight ahead. Bending the knees out or in during execution of the shot will result in poor balance. A slight jump off the floor, coordinated with the release of the ball, will provide extra force for the longer shot.

THE TWO-HAND OVERHEAD SHOT

The two-hand overhead shot is better adapted for use by a big player. Smaller men can use it effectively, however. This shot is made the same as the two-hand chest shot, with the exception of the position of the ball. When the ball is placed above the head, more wrist and finger action is needed to apply the force, as most of the arm action is already expended. The position of the body and the action of the legs and feet is exactly the same as used in the two-hand chest shot. A slight jump can be used to help increase the force for release.

· 8 ·

Skills and Strategies for Passing the Ball

As good shooters are vital for offensive power, good passers are also necessary to penetrate the defense. With good passing and ball handling, along with some consistency in defensive play, a team should never be embarrassed. Shooting skills will vary on different nights and will show inconsistency. Mental hazards which lead to lack of confidence or equipment differences such as lighting will upset a player psychologically. When this happens, his shooting will be affected more than other parts of his game. The skill of making a basket offers more of a problem than the skill used in making a good pass. All other phases of his game such as dribbling, ball handling, and defensive play remain more consistent in spite of upsets that might bother the player otherwise.

Because of the different types of systems in basketball, there are many kinds of passes used. Team passing will vary from the orthodox or conservative to the spectacular. Fancy passes thrill the crowd when they are successful, but most of the time the opponents receive more of these passes than do the teammates. Regardless of the possible types of passes, you should concentrate on teaching the passes that are best adapted to your style of ball. Many coaches insist on hours of practice using drills to perfect passes never used in their particular system. This is wasted time which can be spent more profitably to develop passes used or to work on other skills of the game.

To defeat teams that collapse on defense or use the zone, a successful team must be able to pass the ball well. Good maneuvering should always accompany good passing to get inside the defense. The good shot attempt can only be achieved by excellent passing and maneuvering. The ability to pass the ball in to the post man and also to have good passing in semi-control or control-game attack is of major importance in winning games, or at least in functioning well as a team. You must organize your practice time and include drills to develop this particular offensive technique.

The most common passes used in offensive systems in basketball are these:

Two-handed chest	Two-handed shoulder
Baseball	Two-handed side
Bounce	Back pass
One-handed pro	Drop pass
Semi-hook	Overhead
Hook	Hand-off

In the style of attack we use at Brigham Young University the following passes are taught and we work hard to perfect them to a satisfactory degree of operation:

Two-handed chest	Semi-hook
Bounce	Two-handed shoulder
Baseball	Hand-off

The Two-Handed Chest Pass

Basic to any system of basketball, the two-handed chest pass is used to make short-distance passes. The mechanics of performance allow such movements as fakes and drives, shots and passes. Include the same principles in teaching the two-handed chest pass as you would for the two-handed chest shot. The accuracy of the flight of the ball in the pass and the shot should not vary as the release of the ball off the hands is very much the same.

Give players the following instructions for effecting the two-handed chest pass:

1. Hold the ball in the finger tips, not the palms or heels of the hands.
2. Place the hands on the side of the ball with the fingers spread comfortably and the thumbs parallel.
3. The hands may be held slightly lower than in the two-handed shot.
4. Keep elbows close to the body to assure relaxation of hands and forearms and to avoid a direct release being made by the thumbs.
5. Release the ball entirely with arm extension and wrist and finger action, with a slight spin toward the passer after its release.
6. Aim at the chest of the receiver.
7. If the pass is somewhat long, take a step as the ball is released to assure the necessary force. A left-handed player should step with his right foot and a right-handed player should step with his left foot to get proper body balance and force.
8. In both long and short distance two-handed chest passes, check the extension of the arm with the follow-through coming with the wrist and finger action. The palms of the hands will be facing the floor and the arms should be held momentarily in front and not allowed to swing to either side.

The Bounce Pass

Teach the bounce pass as a follow-up of the two-handed chest pass. The bounce pass is more difficult to execute properly than the two-handed chest pass. The possibilities of the action of the ball off the floor such as the spin of the ball, the release, and floor conditions add to the hazards of this pass. These conditions do not exist when a pass is made directly to another player with the ball

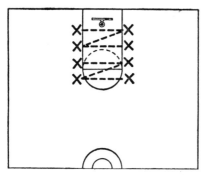

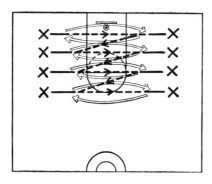

Fig. 169. Standing pass drill for two-handed chest pass. Pass can be made at this distance without a step. Check the details of the pass as the squad works in groups of four. Bounce passes can be introduced with this drill.

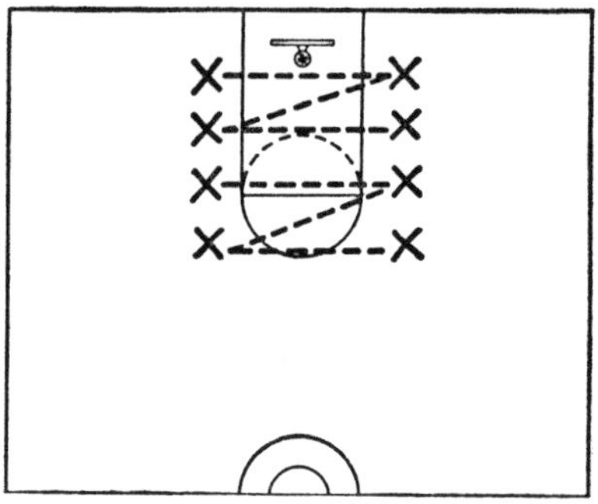

Fig. 170. Same drill with exception of distance of pass. A step must be made by the passer to compensate for distance. Right handers step with left foot; left handers step with right foot. Use this drill for bounce passes, too.

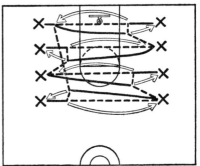

Fig. 171. Running pass drill using the two-handed chest pass. Passer must move opposite ball after pass is made (white arrows). Bounce pass can also be practiced with this drill.

Fig. 172. Running pass drill using the two-handed chest pass with a short return pass to the first passer. A long pass must be made and then a fast cut toward the receiver for a return pass. Passing rhythm is developed along with good ball handling.

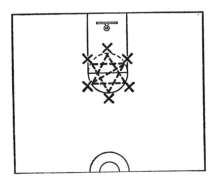

Fig. 173. Circle drill for two-handed
chest pass. Triangles should be used for
passing. Flip pass can be made to next
man. Good competetive drills for groups.
Have losers run laps as penalty.

touching no objects. The pass is made exactly as the two-handed
chest pass including the holding of the ball, the release and the
step toward the target. As a result of the same mechanics being
used, learning capacity will be greater when instruction of this
pass follows the two-handed chest pass.

The different things that need to be watched in the execution of
this pass are the wrist action in release, the bounce target and the
receiving mark. Instruct the player to have a slight roll of the
wrists and fingers forward and over. The wrist roll will give the
ball a slight spin away from the passer. The spin of the ball in
this manner results in faster action off the floor and consequently a
quicker pass. When the ball is released with a spin toward the
passer the bounce of the ball off the floor is much slower. The
forward spin is not enough to make the ball difficult to handle by
the receiver. At no time should you allow your players to use a
side spin or put "English" on the ball. This condition makes the
ball too hard to catch.

The bounce spot should favor distance toward the receiver. If
the bounce target does not do that, the pass is too slow and may

have to bounce twice before reaching the receiver. When all of your squad uses this spin and bounce target they become accustomed to the feel of the ball as it comes in. You will need to teach a different receiving level with this pass. Good bounce passers will put the pass into the receiver at belt buckle or waist level. The waist area is much easier to emphasize for receiving purposes, since a higher target would necessitate a harder bounce and naturally a slower pass. The bounce pass can be used well on the fast break, against big men, feeding the post with a step-out, on a change of direction and give-and-go options. The bounce pass is a necessary pass and certainly an effective one for any style of ball.

You can use the same drills teaching the bounce pass as used in the two-handed chest pass instruction. It is always a good teaching procedure to start with the stationary drills and then proceed to passing to men moving for game purposes. This progressive step in teaching the pass will improve the accuracy of the pass.

The Baseball Pass

The baseball pass is the long pass in basketball and can be used effectively in many situations. Any team using the fast break must be well versed in the use of this pass. It is also operative when an interception is made and a man is down court. The baseball pass is thrown like a catcher's throw to second base or a quarterback's throw in football. Any wind-up motion must be eliminated as it slows the pass.

When teaching the pass, many important points must be shown to the player. You generally assume the ball will always be held at chest level before any pass can be made. Instruct the boy to bring the ball back of the ear with both hands on the ball. From this position the throwing hand and arm is brought farther back and the ball is thrown with an overhand action close to the side of the head. The ball must never be dropped to hip level and then brought up into position as this action wastes time. As the ball is started forward past the ear, the arm is extended in the throwing action. The ball should be released off the finger tips. The fingers should be straight and the palm of the passing hand should be facing the floor at the completion of the pass. The angle of the fingers at the time the ball is released will determine the arch and flight of the ball. Any twisting action of the wrist will result in a side spin of the ball which makes it harder to catch. The side spin of the ball will result in the ball curving instead of going straight. The same result will exist if the throwing motion is made with the arm too far from the side of the head.

The body and legs can help the arm make the longer pass. The passer can step with the opposite foot of the throwing arm to get better balance in the execution of the pass and to increase the force of release. The shoulders and the hips also play an important part in this pass. The target area of the receiver should be in front of the chest so the pass can be taken in stride. Game situations provide for the use of the baseball pass to a moving target. You can begin instruction of this pass with stationary drills. When you proceed to teach longer passes to moving targets, windows are apt to be broken. The ball will have to be retrieved from the bleachers many times in the early stages of the baseball pass drill. In addition to teaching the pass in various drills, you can emphasize the use of the pass in your breakdown drills.

Drills Used to Teach the Baseball Pass

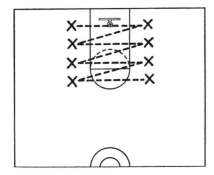 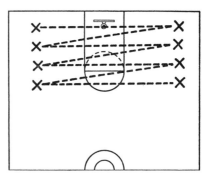

Fig. 174. Close standing drill for teaching baseball pass. Step must be taken with opposite foot as pass is made.

Fig. 175. Second stage of standing drill for baseball pass. Greater distance of pass necessitates step to get more force for throw.

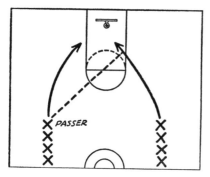 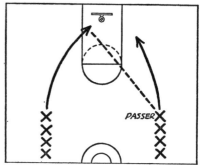

Fig. 176. Baseball pass drill with moving target.

Fig. 177. Baseball pass drill with moving target from opposite side of floor.

The Semi-Hook Pass

The semi-hook pass is similar to the hook pass, but is much faster in execution which makes it more effective. Naturally, this pass must be shorter than the hook pass as it has less arm and shoulder action. We have not taught the hook pass at Brigham Young University for several years. We found that our team members were using it too often at the wrong time. Opponents were blocking the majority of these passes due to the telegraphic aspect as the hand and arm were dropped to make the pass. In years past, the hook pass was commonly used to clear congested areas. Now teams are using the fake and dribble instead.

When teaching the semi-hook pass, you must work on the premise that a good fake must precede the pass. This opens a vulnerable area to make the pass through the opponent. With a fake bounce pass, which causes the opposition to drop his hand, the semi-hook pass is made possible. The pass is made with wrist and finger action off the fake bounce pass to pass over the shoulder region of the opponent. This pass is especially good to feed a post man or get the pass inside the defense. It is a quick pass and can be made accurately with a quick flip to release the ball past the opponent before he can recover from the first fake. When the opponent does not react to the original fake, then the first pass can be made.

The Two-Handed Shoulder Pass

Often your team may have difficulty getting the first pass out on a fast break from the right side of the bankboard. Chances of getting the rebound pass out are better if the rebounder is left handed and can turn to his right and fire a left-handed baseball pass out.

If the right hander is to the right of the basket he must turn to the inside to make the pass, or turn to his right, which presents two disadvantages: he not only must delay the pass, but he also turns into the defense. The two-handed shoulder pass will remedy this problem.

On the left side of the bankboard, the right hander has a natural turnout and is in a good position to clear the first pass. Consequently, the fast break can go well with that opportunity, but will be slowed somewhat unless the two-handed shoulder pass can be perfected for the awkward side.

In executing the two-handed shoulder pass, teach your players the following:

1. Bring the ball over the shoulder with both hands.
2. With a flip of the wrist and fingers as well as an extension of the arms the pass can be made a considerable distance with good accuracy.
3. As the pass is made step with the opposite foot toward the received for good balance and to increase the force of the pass.

Begin the instruction with a standing drill much the same as used in other passes. Have your players approximately ten feet apart to acquire the proper fundamentals of the pass. Extend the distance as the pass instruction progresses. The target area for the pass is the chest of the wing man who is button-hooking from the sideline to receive the outlet pass.

The Hand-Off Pass

When a screening and driving game is used, the hand-off pass becomes a must. It is called the hand-off pass because of its similarity to a quarterback's hand-off passes in football. Post men have the best opportunity to use this pass because of more cutting situations existing off the post. However, this pass can be used by all the team members as it helps to perform the various maneuvers off a screen. Often boys become very clever with this pass by faking one way and passing the other. Faking is the key to good quarterbacking in the "T" formation in football and can become deceptive if enough time is spent to perfect it. The same thing holds true in basketball.

The hand-off pass is made by giving the ball to a teammate from a short distance with a flip or a direct give. It is not a difficult pass to master and because of this it need not be practiced as much as the other passes unless you are concerned with deception. You can teach the fundamentals of this pass in your regular break-down drills, or your game drills. Sometimes you may inherit a post man who can fake and use this pass with a lot of deception. When this occurs you would be amiss not to encourage it.

The pass must be handled with feather touch or "put on a shelf" so to speak, so the cutter can handle the pass easily. As in football, team members can execute this pass well and many times the cutter can take the ball without a concentration of vision on the ball. To take the eyes off the ball on other passes would result in a large number of miscues.

As mentioned previously in this chapter, there are other passes used successfully in basketball systems. In many options the drop pass is used with good results. The drop pass can be used well on an outside play, with the passer dropping the ball and moving in to cut off the defensive man with a moving screen. The back pass and the two-handed side pass made off the hip have been used in some systems with success. The overhead pass is used by a majority of teams. This pass can be more effective when used by taller men in passing over an opponent. When smaller men use it against equal size it must be set up and executed with good faking. The telegraphic obstacle is present in this pass much the same as in the hook pass and as a result it must be preceded with a good fake. The hook pass is used by many teams to clear congested areas. The pro pass is a good pass to use in close areas. It consists of a quick flip with either hand almost simultaneously with receiving the ball.

It cannot cover a great distance as the power required is not there.

In trying to keep your offensive attack simple, use the passes that best fit your attack. Time spent in perfecting the passes best adapted for your play will pay off in the long run. The passing game must be good and the ball handled well to result in a minimum number of mistakes, as bad passes resulting in loss of ball possession are too costly.

Passing Through a Man

Passing would be no problem in basketball if there were no opposition. After teaching your squad the proper fundamentals of passing, you can acquaint them with the techniques of passing through a defensive man. Lob passes would be the answer if they could be made effective. However, lob passes are few in basketball because of the time element involved in the flight of the ball up and down. During the flight of the ball in the lob pass, the defense has an excellent opportunity to converge on the offensive player receiving the pass.

If a player is to succeed in passing through a man, or getting the ball inside the defense, he must be aware of the fakes necessary to do this. He must also know the vulnerable areas to make the pass through. The major passing problem exists when the post man must be hit and the pass executed well for good receiving. Passes to side men are not too difficult when the receiver does his part to make the pass possible. Cross court passes should be held to a minimum because of the chance for interception being greater and the slight chance for defensive recovery by the passing team.

Where Is the Opponent Vulnerable?

An opponent is generally vulnerable at the feet and the shoulder and head areas. The defensive man must be set up with the proper faking to open the zones for the pass. The faking should be done with good rhythm, a count on fakes and passing not to exceed three. For example, when a player fakes a bounce pass, the natural reaction of the opponent results in dropping the hand, arm and shoulder to block the bounce pass possibility. As the opponent makes this adjustment, he becomes open for a pass over the head and shoulder. When the opponent is quick enough to close the head and shoulder zone, the pass can be made at the feet on a rhythm count of three. Where the fake is made at the head and shoulder area, the natural reaction of the opponent is to bring the hand and arm up to stop the pass. The action opens the bounce-pass area at the feet. To fake one direction and pass the same way results in telegraphing the pass and eventual blocking of the pass attempt and possible loss of the ball.

Feeding the Post Man

Passing through a man is most difficult when attempting to pass to post men or get inside a zone defense. Other situations will be present when the pass must be made through a player, but the two situations mentioned will need to be practiced most. If the post man is to receive the pass, he must first get clear. This position must be gained by proper faking and angle cuts which facilitate the player's meeting the pass. A step out with the foot on the side of the defensive player will establish a protective pocket. To be successful, the pass must always be made opposite the defensive man playing your post man. Sometimes a little shuffle hop to meet the ball will add the protection of the body to the pass.

Your hardest teaching assignment in getting outside men to feed the post will be having them make the pass when the post man is free. Some players are natural post feeders and have no trouble getting the pass in. Most players, however, even after hours of drill, have trouble hitting the post man when is is open. Slow reaction delays the pass, permitting the defense to recover. The post man can help the outside passers by using the hand opposite the defensive man as a guide and a target for the passers. Most of the coaches contend the feed into the post from side court is the best. You can have a more versatile attack by feeding from the side and the front.

Feeding the Side Man

Feeding the side player is not too difficult unless the opposition contests the pass in by overplaying your man. When the opponents do this, a reverse pivot after a fake pass or a change of direction on the part of the intended receiver will free him for the pass. You must always insist that your players come to meet the ball. A step toward the ball with the foot on the opposition side will allow protection and open a target off the defense for a safer pass. Such movements as give-and-go, change of direction, reverse pivot, and taking your defensive man to the base line are good to open passing lanes on the side of the floor.

Passing Through Drills

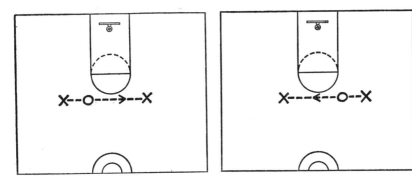

Fig. 178-179. Three-man line drill. The X players are about 15 feet apart. The O player must be aggressive and force the pass. No lob passes allowed. X players must stay within an area about 5 feet wide.

You can teach passing through by using three men in a group. The passer and the receiver should be about fifteen feet apart. The third player is placed between the passer and receiver to contest the passes made by each of the other two. The middle man must be aggressive and force the pass. To be passive and set in front of the intended receiver kills the drill since the pass is impossible to make. The ball must be passed through the man and never lobbed over him. Both passers must make their pass in a restricted area to either side of them. When the middle man touches or deflects the pass, the passer responsible for the poor pass goes inside and the middle man takes the passer's place in the line.

Fig. 180. Bull pen drill. Passing tri-angles. Man passing must never lob or pass to man next to him.

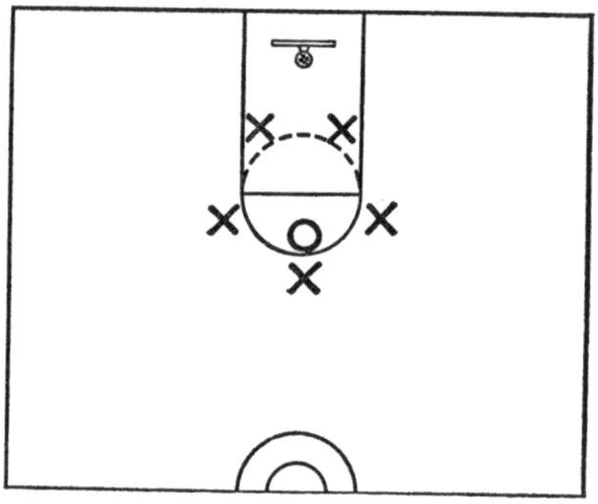

Fig. 181. Bull pen drill. O represents man in middle. He must be aggressive following the ball and play the man with the ball.

The circle drill is also effective in teaching passing through. The circle drill is best when six players make up the group. With the six players one man can be placed in the center of the circle giving the other five good triangle passes. The restraining circles for the jump ball offer a good sized restraining area. Place your boys just outside the circle for good passing conditions. The middle man must be aggressive and force the pass. The circle men cannot lob the ball over the middle man. Neither can they pass to the man next to them. These allowances would not add to the desired results. Whenever the middle man touches or deflects the pass, the passer responsible for the mistake must take his place inside the circle. These two drills make for fun and competition and conse-quently help your squad become better passers. All the boys try to keep from playing inside the circle, thereby becoming conscious of good passes.

Always impress upon your team members the importance of good passing. Keep accurate statistics on all bad passes, violations and other mistakes that will cause your team to lose possession of the ball. These statistics should be kept for all scrimmages and games. Inform your players that each bad pass or violation that surrenders the ball costs you four points. Your team will lose a chance for two points and the opposition gains a chance for two points. Good passing and ball handling contribute a great deal to your chances of becoming a winner.

Ball Handling

The pass receiver is, of course, just as responsible in making a pass successful as the passer. While the passer must be hitting the mark to make receiving possible, the receiver must adhere to certain principles to catch the ball successfully. In the majority of cases when a receiver fumbles the ball, he is taking his eyes off the ball momentarily to determine the position of the opponent. However, he may be trying to receive the ball with double vision—one eye on the ball and one eye on the opponent. Constantly remind your players to "look the ball into the hands." After a player receives the ball he can work on keeping the attack going. When a boy keeps his eye on the ball and the pass is good, fumbling will be greatly decreased.

In addition to watching the ball into the hands, the receiver must not fight the ball. He can avoid this by cushioning the ball with a slight give of the fingers, wrists and elbows. The ball should never be caught with the palm or heel of the hand. Fingertip action, feel and control are just as important in passing and catching as they are in shooting. With a slight cushioning action, the ball can be received easier and fumbling overcome somewhat. In this situation, have your players learn the proper position of the hands in catching the ball. For all passes above the waist (where they should be), have them catch the ball with the thumbs inside and the palms of the hands toward the ball. When the pass is made below the hips, have them catch the ball with the little fingers together on the inside and the palms of the hands facing toward the ceiling.

MAJOR CAUSES OF FUMBLING

Eyes Off the Ball

If a boy is to catch the ball he must certainly see it. Without concentration on the ball as it comes toward the receiver, fumbles will be too plentiful. Football coaches will paint numbers on the ball and have the player call the number on the ball as he receives the pass. This will help to overcome looking away at the time the ball is caught. Numbers or colors on the basketball could help to overcome the weakness of taking the eyes off the ball in catching. Passing drills with a constant reminder to look the ball into the hands at all times is needed to correct this weakness.

Pass Too Hard

The hard pass is rather a common mistake many players make. They have the idea they must "burn" the ball into a man and consequently the receiver cannot handle it. The hard pass is more common with shorter passes. Verbal reminders such as "cushion it," "put feathers on it," or "lay it on a shelf" will help to keep the squad aware of the need for proper speed on passes. The mental attitude of the player is important for cooperation in making the passes the right tempo. If the boy insists on passing the ball too hard, drills will not help to correct this fault. The solution is on the bench instead of on the floor.

Pass Too High or Too Low

Often situations in a game will require perfect timing of everything if a play is to go all the way. A poor passing target results in slowing a player sufficiently to permit the defense to recover. A pass that is too high or too low resulting in a fumble or a delay in passing or shooting will be the difference in scoring and not scoring. The receiving mark must be emphasized at all times and every effort made to hit it with good passes. Always emphasize the chest area as the best target. If the player is moving, the ball should be placed in front of the chest to make it possible for the receiver to take the pass without breaking his running stride. It always helps the passer if the receiver places his hands in the position in front of the upper trunk to form a target. This procedure is similar to the catcher in baseball helping his pitcher with a mark at which to aim.

Pass with Too Much Spin

The spinning pass is probably the most difficult to catch unless a boy has had a lot of practice with it. Only the natural spin of the ball should be used in the proper release. Too many times the spin pass occurs when a player turns his wrist in the release or causes the ball to come off the side of the hand. Teaching proper fundamentals of release with periodic checks will help to alleviate faulty spin. Spin passes should not be a problem but you need to be aware of the possibility and quickly correct it before it grows and becomes commonplace with all the passes.

Poor Vision

This condition should probably assume the number one spot in importance in any part of the game. If a boy cannot see, his value to the team will be null. It certainly could be a problem that might be overlooked on the assumption the boy's vision has been tested in other programs. Youngsters may have poor vision and not be aware of it. While coaching in high school the writer had a player who squinted his eyes every time he caught the ball. He fumbled the ball more often than he caught it. Poor vision was suspected and the boy was questioned about his eyes. His answer was honest and sincere when he said he didn't know about his vision but assumed it was good.

To solve the problem the youngster was given a test with the regular eye reading chart. He was found to be almost blind in one eye. Further questioning revealed that the boy was hit in the eye with a shot from a B.B. gun when he was small. Nothing was suspected in the way of poor vision as he assumed his eyesight was all right. When the boy was fitted with the proper glasses a new world was revealed to him. Incidentally, he also overcame his squinting and fumbling.

Every boy on your squad should have his vision tested as part of the pre-practice physical examination. Boys may use unbreakable glasses or contact lenses to overcome the handicaps of poor vision. Players have found these aids satisfactory and have gained confidence through the use of them. Otherwise they would not experience the many opportunities presented by participation in sports. It is always amusing to have boys with good vision do things we expect of players with poor vision. Fun and jesting at this time helps to relieve tension and pressures.

Improper Lead

Brigham Young University lost a very important ball game a few years ago because of an improper lead pass. During this important game with Niagara in the N. I. T. our opponents were leading us by a score of 74-73 in the closing seconds of the game. A fast break opportunity developed for us off an interception. Our lead man was well in front of the defense when the pass was made to him. The pass was slightly short and our player had to break his speed and stride to reach back for the pass. Delay was sufficient to let our opponents recover and gain defensive position costing us a setup opportunity as well as the game. A coach can gain consolation from a play like this by second guessing the possibility and accepting the thought that the player might have missed the setup anyway. Several times since we have lost a chance to score when a pass has been too long or behind the receiver.

Off Balance

Poor balance can exist with both the passer and receiver. You must pay particular attention to this fault and insist on good body balance at all times. Catching the ball off balance necessitates adjustment before any execution of play occurs. Adjustment delay will always benefit the defense. Everything must be ready to strike quickly to gain any advantage the defense will give you. Poor balance will never pay off in basketball.

The Responsibility of the Receiver

The receiver is as much at fault sometimes as the passer. Tell your boys to go get the pass when it is near them. Aggressive pass receiving will make a stronger team. Often times the "alibier" will place the blame for an error on someone else when he is at fault. Drill and statistical records will help to put responsibility on the receiver to get free, to stretch to get the pass and move quickly to catch the ball. Most boys will accept the challenge and the responsibility to work harder for the ball. The player must be able to think as well as move his feet to get this particular assignment completed.

BALL HANDLING DRILLS

Special passing drills will contribute to improving ball handling. These drills can be the peripheral passing drill, pass against the wall, the circle and bull-pen drill, the three-man weave and the five-man weave handoff drills.

The Peripheral Passing Drill

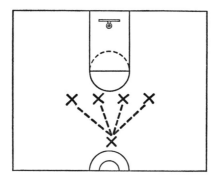

Fig. 182. Peripheral passing drill with two balls. Single man and one member of the line start with a ball.

The peripheral passing drill will serve two purposes. Ball handling and reaction will be helped along with developing some peripheral or side vision which is so important in the game. A boy whose vision is restricted to a straight line is no good on the basketball court. He is like a race horse with blinders since he cannot see the overall development of playing situations. In setting up the drill, use five players to a group with two basketballs. Place four men in a line facing one man at a distance of approximately 10 feet. The four men must be separated so they have 12 or 18 inches between them. One of the four men has a ball as well as the single player facing him.

The purpose of the drill is to have the single man handle the passes of the four men. Care must be taken to avoid catching or passing two balls at the same time. Starting the drill slowly and increasing the tempo as the boys learn to pass is the best procedure. Good sense and reasoning on the part of the participants must exist or the drill will be no good. Your team can have a lot of fun with this drill, and the boy in the single passing position will develop passing and catching skills as well as improve his side vision. Rotate the boys so that each one has a chance to be in the single position before the drill ends. Be careful not to have this activity continue too long.

Pass Against the Wall Drill

Have your poor passers and ball handlers use the wall pass drill often before practice or out of season. It is a very good drill and

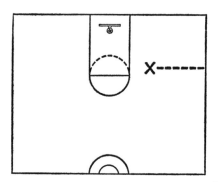

Fig. 183. Passing against the wall drill. Single player throws ball against wall and catches rebounds.

weaknesses can be helped by the person needing the special attention. The player can practice this drill by himself, which means he can do it almost any time. Recommend that the boy take a position between 5 and 10 feet from a wall and throw the ball against the wall and receive it for several minutes each day. His skill improves by doing and he must do it well for increase of efficiency. Flipping the ball from hand to hand will also develop the feel and touch necessary to become a better ball handler.

The Circle and Bull-Pen Drill

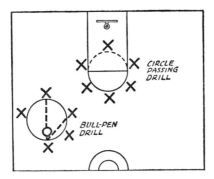

Fig. 184. Passing triangles with man contesting in center.

The circle and bull-pen drills have been treated previously in the text. Both drills will contribute to good passing and ball handling.

The Three-Man Weave

The three-man weave passing drill affords the opportunity for practicing long passes, short passes and handoffs. Start the ball in the middle line and have the passer go behind the receiver and also

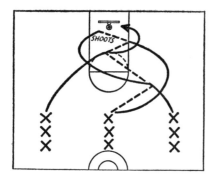
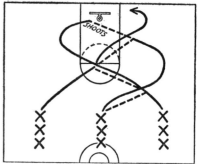

Fig. 185. Three-man weave. Pass and go behind.

Fig. 186. Three-man weave. Pass and go in front.

in front of him. These directions must be exact to prevent collisions. Designate the number of passes to be made before the shot is taken. You can have the group start with six passes and increase the passes to twelve before shooting the ball. The long and close maneuvers afford enjoyment and the squad will get a kick out of this drill and improve its skills at the same time. After using the pass and go-behind maneuver, have your players pass and go in front. The change of movement requires some thought and is good to help them adjust and practice flexibility in the attack. This latter movement also conforms with the movement of the weave and helps to develop the options as well as to improve ball handling.

The drill is practiced best from mid-court to the basket. Three lanes of players establish the beginning forces necessary. The middle man can start the play either way and move in front or in behind the wing man after the pass. Have the players interchange lines so practice can be achieved from each position.

The Five-Man Weave

Adding two more men to the three-man weave will result in the five-man weave passing drill. With five men participating the

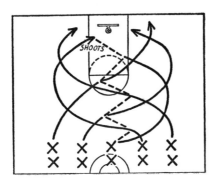

Fig. 187. Five-man weave. Pass and go
behind only.

passer must go behind two men after passing to keep the drill balanced. Never run this drill with the passer going in front of the receiver as it will be too crowded and the results will be poor. Start this drill with the middle man going either way. Starting at mid-court and working toward the basket will allow two groups to participate. This organization will give more practice to each individual. Both the three-man weave and the five-man weave serve as good conditioners in early season. Use these two passing drills as fun drills toward the end of the season to provide an opportunity to break away from routine and monotony.

· 9 ·

Teaching the How and When of Dribbling

Coach Paul McBrayer of Eastern Kentucky once commented, "The boy dribbled until he found trouble." Dribbling can be over-done. Unless each player knows how, and equally as important *when* to dribble, your team will find trouble. If used to extreme, dribbling results in individualism and lack of team play that is essential in winning games.

Pointers on Teaching the Dribble

Before looking at situations in which dribbling is more effective than passing, let's consider what a player must learn to be a good dribbler. Some tips on coaching your team in dribbling follow:

1. Bend the body slightly at the hips with head up, eyes focused ahead of the play and not on the ball. The player who watches the ball will miss many team openings down court simply because he does not see the developments.

2. Distribute weight of the body on the balls of the feet, with knees bent slightly, allowing for quick and agile movement.

164

3. Bounce the ball with a pumping action of the hand, wrist and arm. Never slap or fight the ball.

4. Spread the fingers of the dribbling hand slightly and keep them straight.

5. Wrist movement should be semi-locked so that the hand and fingers do not drop down. Otherwise dribbling is slowed because the hand has to be brought up to effect the pumping action.

6. Never carry the ball by placing your dribbling hand underneath it. This violation means loss of possession.

7. For best results as a dribbler, the player should learn to use both hands. This prevents the defense from forcing a player by overplaying him.

8. When teaching beginners to dribble, have them practice the fundamentals in a small area, maneuvering only slightly to get the feel of the ball. After mastering the dribble in a restricted area, they can tackle the variations necessary for good operation.

High and Low Dribble

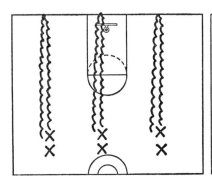 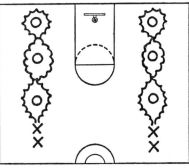

Fig. 188. High dribble for speed. Relay competition. Both hands used. Dribble down with right hand and back with left. Use full court.

Fig. 189. Low dribble for protection and change of direction. Opponent is stationary.

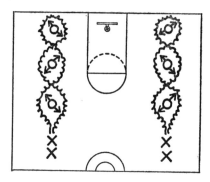

Fig. 190. Low dribble for protection
and change of direction. Opponent may
take one step and try to get ball.

There are two types of dribble: the high dribble which you need
for speed in bringing the ball down the floor or driving for the
basket, and the low dribble which is needed for protection. The
high dribble should be bounced between the knee and the hip
area, the low dribble at knee level or lower.

Players must know the need and use of these two variations.
Otherwise the opposition will more easily steal the ball. Alertness
and agility when dribbling are vital. Caution a player always to
protect a dribble by keeping his body between the opponent and the
ball. If he dribbles facing his opponent with the ball in front of him,
not only does he increase chances of losing the ball, but he looks
inferior because the opponent is more of a threat.

Variations of the Dribble

In addition to the ability to dribble well, both high and low, a
player must develop the ability to maneuver with the dribble. Such
maneuvers as change of pace, change of direction, and reverse
dribble will help to elude an opponent. Fancy dribbling—such as
behind the back or under the leg—should be discouraged. In most
cases, these trick operations will backfire and your opponents will

gain possession of the ball. After a player has learned to dribble well in a straight line, using both hands, and using high and low methods, he should advance to maneuvering drills.

Change of Pace Dribble

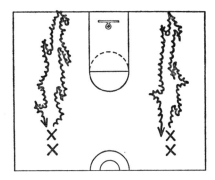

Fig. 191. Change of pace dribbling drill. No opposition. Use right hand down and left back.

Change of pace dribble is just what it states—a variation of fakes, starts, and stops with several speeds. Dribbling fast, slowing down, or retreating a little causes the opponents to overplay; and a burst of speed at the opportune time will enable the dribbler to break away from his man. Several players have mastered the change of pace with excellent results. Fouls may be committed by the defense trying to play a clever dribbler. Any defensive man slow in footwork can be eluded with a change of pace dribble. Sometimes on a fast break the middle man can use this dribbling maneuver to cause the defense to spread out as he slows down anticipating the pass to the side man converging on the basket. As the defense spreads the dribbler can pick up speed and go all the way for the easy basket before the opponents can recover position.

This specialty in basketball is similar to the work of a good pitcher, who can have the batter swinging a certain tempo at his fast ball. The cross-up with a change of pace pitch will usually leave the batter hanging at the plate. The same maneuver is used in football by the elusive halfback who gives a tackler a leg and with a change of pace takes the leg away and leaves the tackler on the ground empty handed. Change of pace practice should include dribbling forward, backward and at various angles with changes of speed. After a player has mastered the change up without opposition, have someone play him to steal the ball and keep defensive position. This drill will help the dribbler develop the use of both hands with confidence and also teach him to protect the ball with his body and the low bounce. The change of pace dribble is an excellent tactic in a fast break dribble or on a one-on-one when the opponent is forcing.

Change of Direction Dribble

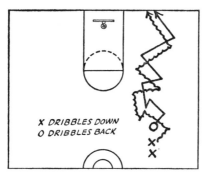 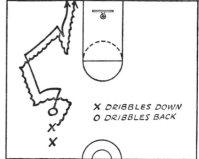

X DRIBBLES DOWN
O DRIBBLES BACK

X DRIBBLES DOWN
O DRIBBLES BACK

Fig. 192. Change of pace and change of direction drill with opposition. Opponent plays position on this drill.

Fig. 193. Change of pace and change of direction drill with opposition. Opponent plays position and also tries to steal ball.

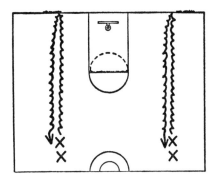

Fig. 194. Forward and backward dribbling drill. Dribble down forward and
back backward. Use right hand down
and back, then left hand down and back.

The dribbler who cannot change direction sharply is handicapped.
A defensive player, if he is of equal ability, takes advantage of the
dribbler who can move only one way or in a straight line.

The change of direction dribble is accomplished as follows:

1. With a good fake and crossover dribble, go one way.
2. Come back immediately to the starting position.
3. Then with the same crossover dribble, go the other way.

While practicing this change of direction dribble, the players
must not carry the ball. Pressure near the top of the ball favoring
the side is required for the crossover technique. Some players attempt this action with a good head fake. If the opponent is smart,
he will not be fooled with this faking. As a result, the feet must be
used along with head when faking.

To make the crossover more effective, some change of pace
must be used. For example, if the dribbler is using a righthand
dribble, he may be dribbling straight or slightly to his right. Suddenly a step with the left foot to the player's left, at the same time
cutting the ball across close to the legs, will leave the defensive
man still moving to his left. If the defensive man steps with your

player on the crossover, then an immediate comeback to the dribbler's right side will evade the defense. When the opponent plays for the comeback a continuation of direction will result in getting free. During execution of this action, inform your squad that the ball must be kept close to the body on the crossover. Getting the ball too far in front will enable the defense to steal it.

Reverse Dribble

The reverse dribble action can be used profitably when the opponent becomes overanxious to steal the ball. In most cases the opposition will try to overplay your dribbler in one direction or the other in his attempt to steal the ball. A reverse pivot off the inside foot with a change of dribble to the other hand leaves the defense out of position. When your player is dribbling to his left the defensive man will be forcing him in front and to his left side. Using a quick stop and pivot on the right foot, the dribbler can pick up the ball with the right hand, and the left foot becomes the lead foot as he reverses direction and moves to his right. Maneuvers such as this will leave the opponent clearly out of position and open the way for a drive to the basket. As in the change of direction drill, check the dribbler out on the reverse pivot so that he doesn't carry the ball and commit a violation.

Every player on your squad should know how to use the dribble and its variations effectively.

Should You Pass or Dribble?

People concerned with basketball contend, and rightly, that the pass is much faster than the dribble and should always be used in preference. In most cases this is true, but there are certain specific times when the dribble is preferable. These situations are as follows:

1. Three-on-two or a two-on-one fast break opportunity.
2. The drive in to the basket.
3. The control game.
4. Bringing the ball down the floor.
5. Clearing congested areas.
6. Setting up play patterns.

Each player should know these opportunities and should know how to use the proper dribble for each occasion. Players should never use the dribble unless an advantage can result.

Some players develop a habit of bouncing the ball after receiving a pass or before they shoot. Such a habit eliminates the opportunity to be a threat with the ball. When your player uses his dribble while standing still, he becomes "dead" and the defense can play him tighter and force him to pass off or be tied up. With the dribble opportunity remaining after a pass has been received, the defense will have to play off your man. In the event the defense elects to play tight with the dribble not used, your player can easily foil the defensive man to advance the attack.

Dribble on the Fast Break

After a missed shot is rebounded and the fast break is started with a pass to the wing man, every attempt should be made to get the ball to the middle man as quickly as possible. The middle man can cause the defense to commit itself sooner when he uses the dribble down the floor. Timing both types of fast break attack, the pass down the floor is slightly faster than the dribble. Cross passing, however, helps the defense to drop back and zone the basket forcing the offense to take a longer shot. When the dribble is used in the center of the attack, with the wing men converging to the basket, the defense has to stop the dribbler. Otherwise, he can get a good shot unmolested or go all the way for a lay-up. If your offensive strategy and execution can force the opponent out to play the dribbler, it will open the area for the wing man to cut toward the basket. Opening the defense by forcing them to play a certain man will offer a better shot opportunity. When the defense uses a tandem, the worst shot your team can get will be from the free throw line. Your player might have to shoot from the line when the defense zones your fast break.

Clearing Congested Areas

Congested areas develop around the backboard after the ball has been retrieved. As the opponent closes in, your player will have to fake and dribble to the side to clear the first pass out. If your player is double teamed, the ball will have to be cleared with a pass. With a minimum loss of manpower the defense may force your rebounder to the corner or double team him. Your fast break will be slowed down by this maneuver on the part of your opponent. Most of the dribbles in congested areas have to be set up with fakes if there is a chance to break into the less crowded space.

The Drive In

With proper faking on a one-on-one situation, your player may get the defensive man to step toward him permitting your man to dribble in for the layup. Sometimes the defensive man will attempt to overplay to force direction. A comeback with the dribble will find the way open toward the basket. On a long pass down the floor or after an interception, the dribble will have to be used to get into the basket area and capitalize on the easy shot.

The Control Game

Many teams use an excellent dribbler for their control game. The other four men on the team are waived to the side lines to permit the clever dribbler to operate with an open center. When he can evade his defensive man, he opens the way to drive in forcing other members of the defense to compensate and leave their men. If the defense does not use this strategy the dribbler can go in to score. Clever dribbling will draw many fouls in the control game as the opposition is forced to gamble and will overplay in trying to stop the dribbling tactics. Being members of a team that specializes in this control game, and meeting the dribbling requirements, creates an opportunity for players to earn their award and at the same time get part of their tuition paid. Some teams use players with special abilities for spot performances such as this.

Bringing the Ball Down the Floor

When bringing the ball down the floor, the dribble is both faster and less risky than cross passes. However, if the opponent presses, a combination of dribbling and passing can be employed. With an effective dribble your team can maneuver your opponent out of position on a one-on-one.

Setting Up Options

When you use a weave or a clear-out option, the dribble is a good weapon. On most weave patterns a one or two bounce dribble is generally necessary for proper maneuvering. The ability of a player to dribble down the side to draw the defense out, or to permit teammates to clear the side, will also help your offensive attack.

· 10 ·

How to Coach Individual Offensive Maneuvers

After practicing the various individual offensive techniques, you can now consider a combination of some of these techniques. Most of these maneuvers will be possible when a one-on-one situation exists. Through proper faking and setting up of continuities, these opportunities are always present. The maneuvers will have to be coordinated differently against different defenses, to produce results.

In your effort to win games, remember that out-smarting your opponent is of prime importance. In case you can make your opponents commit themselves into a defensive lapse or a movement mistake, the development will allow your team to move quickly and decisively. You should drill your players to recognize the defensive error and capitalize on it. This is accomplished partially through much drill on quick reaction maneuvers. Mastering these maneuvers will greatly increase a player's efficiency in basketball.

Give-and-Go

The give-and-go maneuver is very old but still effective. It has been very popular in the systems employed by teams in the eastern part of the United States. An open center or plenty of room to

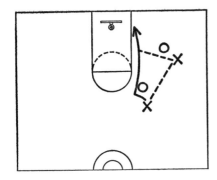

Fig. 195. Give and go on side.

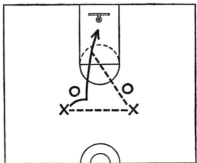

Fig. 196. Give and go in front.

maneuver is conducive to give-and-go action. Two possibilities present opportunities to use this technique. The "swivel head" defense affords one possibility. Some teams will have a player of the "swivel head" type. Scouts are always alert for this particular defensive weakness and teams are prepared to take advantage of it. The "swivel head" is so called because he takes his eyes off his man to follow the flight of the ball. As a result of this, the movement of the offensive man he is assigned to is neglected. As the eyes of the defensive player are focused on the flight of the ball, the offensive man can break toward the basket for a return pass to go all the way or force the defense into a two-on-one.

The other possibility for a give-and-go is present when the defense is playing its men tight. Proper maneuvers by the offense will permit certain advantages. Sometimes speed alone will be sufficient. The defensive team may be as fast and as smart as your team, however, and will play orthodox position by loosening after the pass has been made. A change of pace or change of direction may free your man for a give-and-go. During practice a two-on-two drill will help your team develop these two movements. A pass and a quick break toward the basket will enable your player to free himself when the defense gambles with a tight position in order to harass your play. Maneuvers similar to give-and-go can be practiced off these drills. Good instruction will include a reverse pivot when the opponent uses pressing tactics to contest the pass in. A cutaway pattern may be used to prepare the squad for a switching man-to-man defense.

Fake and Drive

Every one-on-one permits good faking to create more problems for the defense. Faking action is more successful when accompanied by some movement. Head and shoulder faking is usually insufficient to force the defense to commit. That is, of course, if the opponent is as smart as your player, which is the trend presently. A step in the direction of the defense and the basket accompanied by a head and shoulder fake will cause your opponent to move to counteract the action. When the defense steps toward your team member, a crossover and drive in the direction opposite to the first step is made possible. The first step on the part of the offensive player must be a short jab step of about twelve to fourteen inches. The fake and step should always be toward the defensive man. A step to the side or rear of your player will be wasted time and effort. The first step must always be short so recovery can be made quickly off the jab step. The second step crossing over must be longer and executed quickly to evade the opponent. The second step is the deciding factor in determining possible advantage. The ball must be protected on the dribble by the pocket formed as the crossover step is made. To fake and step with one foot on the jab, and gain distance toward the basket with the other foot, is a violation and should not be allowed.

The defense may step back from your player, which is basically the correct defensive movement. When this occurs, have your man come back with a quick step to resume position for a shot over the opponent. The shot can be made in close with a one-hand attempt or farther from the basket with a two-hand shot. It is probable that the defensive man will remain stationary or over-play the offensive man. If this happens, instruct your players to go on the first fake and drive in the same direction. In the execution of the head-and-shoulder fake accompanied with the jab step, the defense is forced to do something to adjust. When the defense reacts to any movement, the offensive player can always retaliate with a maneuver designed to counter the action of the defense. Practice these maneuvers with two players working together. Moving in both directions must be practiced in order to prevent opponents from forcing one way by over-playing and making your man go to his weak side. Giving the opposition this advantage will result in less effective play and prolonged agony during the game. If you have good shooters who can master driving techniques, the defense will be talking to themselves before the game is very old. In the event the defense plays tight to block the shot, the drive is possible. If they loosen to stop your driving game the shot over is made available. When each member of your team learns these important maneuvers, the defensive assignments will be more difficult to fill and your attack will be hard to stop.

Fake Shot and Drive

With the majority of defenses collapsing on post men or using zone tactics, the fake shot and drive becomes a possibility. When the ball is moved rapidly by the offense against either of these defenses, there must be movement of men by the defense to stop the shooting attack. Inasmuch as the ball can be passed much faster than men can move, the recovery of movement on the part of the defense is oftentimes delayed. Due to this delayed recovery, the shooter will have sufficient time to get his shot away.

The rapid movement makes the defensive man rush more and gamble more in an attempt to block the shot. Try to get the defensive man on his toes to slap at the ball, or cause him to leave his feet and jump to block the shot. The eagerness of the opponent permits a fake shot and drive under for a closer attempt at the basket. The maneuver works better when the lanes are opened by making the defensive man commit himself. Again, your team must remember to recognize the situation immediately and take advantage of it before the defense can recover. When the good shot cannot be secured with this maneuver, the way may be opened for a teammate by forcing the defense to adjust and drop off the first threat.

Drive and Bait

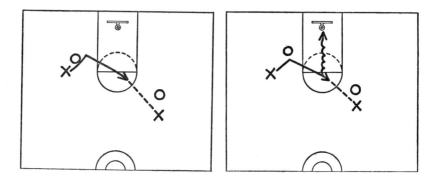

Fig. 197. Drive and bait shooting option.   **Fig. 198.** Drive and bait driving option.

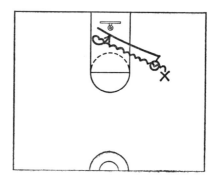

Fig. 199. Drive and bait off dribble when defense forces in front of basket. This maneuver must be preceded by a shot attempt off this drive.

By using an open center attack or by exploiting the weak-side possibilities of the single-post system, the drive and bait will pay dividends. The movement is best adapted for a man coming from a corner or the side to receive a pass. To perform this pattern, a player should be ambidextrous around the foul line or closer to the basket. Breaking from the corner will be set up with a baseline start and a quick angle break toward the passer. The action will free your man for a shot around the free-throw area. The drive and bait can also be used when the defense forces the offensive man out and across in front of the basket on a dribble. To set up these maneuvers the player should be able to make a basket in the direction he is moving with a half-turn pivot shot. When the basket attempt is successful on this move, the defense is prepared for the bait. The defense will have a tendency to overplay the shooter the next time the maneuver is made. The base line start and the change of direction should free the player for the pass in.

When the pass is received the shooter goes through the same motion as the previous attempt to a certain stage. The lead foot is placed as if to pivot for the shot. A head and shoulder fake is made to add to the movement. As the defensive man expects a repeat performance of the first shot, he is drawn into overplaying the shooter on the favored shot side. With the overplay by the defense, the offensive player can reverse pivot and be free for a drive in or a shot. Care must be taken with the head and shoulder fake to protect the ball from being stolen. The ball should be brought up in front of the shoulder but never above the shoulder. This position protects the ball and at the same time gives the appearance of the ball being brought all the way for the shot.

Where the player comes off the baseline the pattern must be made without using the dribble before the fake and shot. Sometimes on a dribble the defense will force your player in front of the basket and beyond it. The drive and bait can be used well at this time if the area is close to the basket. The shot must be attempted the first time this movement is used to establish the bait. With the opponent attempting to play the shot on either situation, the bait and dribble or the bait and shot become possible. When the defense hesitates to play the bait and dribble or the bait and shot, the shot and the dribble in are possible. Keep your opponents guessing at all times for several options are possible from this maneuver.

The Jump Shot Off the Dribble

As mentioned previously, the jump shot off the dribble is the toughest to defense in present day basketball. An offensive player will need space to maneuver and drive the defensive opponent in a direction toward the basket. The defensive player, if he is playing correctly, will in most cases move backward as a first direction on a fake. From this initial movement he will then try to force your man to the side or the end line. This will give your offensive man an angle drive toward the basket with a dribble. The defense must retreat and attempt to force. By retreating and forcing, the defense will block the drive to the basket. The defense never knows, however, when the offense will place both feet hard and come up with a jump shot. Because of this execution, the defense never has a chance to recover to block the shot attempt. The jump shot may also be used off screens, in post play, and outside from a medium distance. A standing jump shot, even though it is hard to stop, is much easier to defense than the jump shot off the dribble. In a case of mismatching of men a taller man would have an advantage with a standing jump shot over a shorter opponent. Again a condition is created when more than one opportunity exists to capitalize on a defensive move.

Fake and Reverse Pivot

The fake and reverse pivot works very well when a team uses a variation of post attacks. It must be set up when the defense allows the opportunity. In most cases, the maneuver can be worked efficiently when the defense tries to force the play. This is especially true when the pivot man moves toward the ball and away from the basket. In other words, when the defensive man is breathing on the neck of your player, the latter will be able to fake and reverse pivot. As the pivot man moves out, he must use good faking tactics to set this up. A fake shot attempt or a fake direction maneuver with a comeback opposite the fake will draw the defense into the

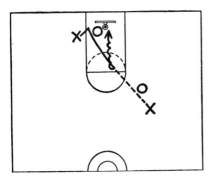 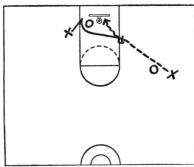

Fig. 200. Fake and reverse pivot with front feed. Fig. 201. Fake and reverse pivot with side feed.

trap. When the defense is playing close, all the post man has to do is reverse and go after receiving the ball.

Some coaches use the terminology of "fake and wheel" in describing the movement. Your post man can work this technique well within the free-throw area as the result has to be determined quickly. To attempt the fake and reverse pivot farther out will lessen the effectiveness of this maneuver as the defense will have time to move to regain good position. Again, as the defense tightens play, the opportunity to fake and wheel is present. When the defense plays loose, the shot opportunity will develop in the 15-foot area as the defense hesitates. This position on the playing floor offers a good shooting range where accuracy percentages can be helped.

Drive, Recoil and Shoot

The drive, recoil and shoot maneuver is more effective when used close to the basket because of the type of shot attempted. The area is inside the free-throw line or on an angle line from the free-throw line to the corner. The jump shot off the dribble has replaced this maneuver somewhat, but it can still be effective if worked right to cause defensive problems. The short distance enables a quicker shot and the force needed for the shot is not as great. The action must be performed facing the basket and the defensive man. Faking is the important factor in setting this up. The step must be made toward the defense as if the player was going to drive in. As the defensive man retreats to protect position, the offensive man can come back with a rocker step and with a slight jump off one foot get his shot away. The defensive man who has retreated slightly to block the drive fake can not recover sufficiently to block the shot. Most defenses will attempt to keep the ball away from any men in this close area. Again, faking and angle cutting are necessary to free men long enough to enable the pass to come in. In many congested areas, clearouts to enable passes in on a situation like this are ideal. The additional space will permit operation of these maneuvers in the usually restricted area.

Pivot Footwork and Details

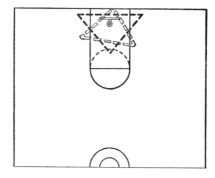

Fig. 202. Pivot footwork in triangle areas off base line for front feed and side feed.

You will need to teach your post man several movements to free himself in the pivot area. The majority of defenses are so concentrated on stopping good pivot men that young men playing that position have to learn more and work harder than other personnel. When your post man operates near the basket, the defense will probably play in front of him to try and keep the ball away from him. As your pivot operator moves out from the basket, the defense will play him three-quarters on the side of the ball to prevent passes in. When your post player is unable to use fakes and direction changes he can easily be defensed and will probably never get in good position. Without good position, the pass to him is impossible to make. He may have to set a high-post position at the free-throw line where the defense will play behind him making the pass in possible. If the defense forces your post man out, his shooting and rebounding effectiveness is reduced. Using the various fakes, angle cuts, and comebacks, the post man can evade defensive men, providing other team members help to keep good floor balance.

When your center maneuvers in circles he is not very effective and the defense will cause him trouble without too much effort. Working in triangles off the base line and toward the free throw line will cause the defense to adjust more to your pivot man's action. This situation requires learning to move without the ball and to get open long enough to allow the feeders to get the pass into the post. Oftentimes your post man will work hard to get free and still not receive the pass. The creates a feeling of "why work hard to get free if the pass is not made?" Avoid a situation like this by instilling in your boys the thought that by working hard all the time they will force an opening somewhere. The maximum effort on the part of all team members will contribute to readiness when the opportunity comes and will help prevent muffing it.

Footwork to Evade Tight Defensive Men

When the defense sets up to contest all passes in to the side men or the opposite front man, your team will have to be able to combat the strategy. In the event the defensive player employs "diver" tactics to steal the ball, or presses to force your players out, chances of receiving the ball are decreased. Continuing to move out for the pass forces your offense to set up too far from the basket. The advantage will be with the defense if it can force you to do this. Wing men will have to be taught several maneuvers to keep the defense from forcing the play. In working with the feeder, the wing man can step out as if to receive the pass. The feeder co-

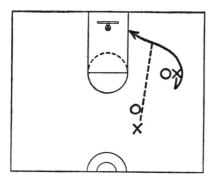

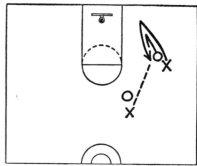

Fig. 203. Footwork to evade tight defense on side man. Defense playing "diver" tactics to intercept pass allows X to reverse pivot and gain position. Front man must fake pass to draw "diver" out.

Fig. 204. Fake to base line and come to meet pass.

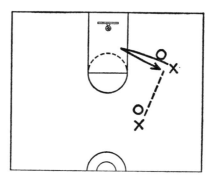

Fig. 205. Fake to free throw area and come to meet pass.

operates by faking pass action to the wing man. As the "diver" moves in to intercept the proposed pass, the wing man can reverse pivot and drive for the basket. The defensive man finds himself out of position and the pivot action by the offense opens the lane. The feeder can then make the pass in to the wing man driving for the basket. The wing man can go all the way to the basket or force the defense to switch. When the defensive man is not a "diver" your player will have to take him to the base line and cut out sharply to meet the ball. Taking the opponent straight across the floor toward the free-throw area and breaking back quickly to receive the pass will achieve the same purpose. Insist that your team members never move out without faking or changing up if the defense is closely contesting all men.

When the front men are being pressed by the defense, care must be taken to avoid cross passes. Movement on the part of the man without the ball must be effective. When you are concerned with this problem, have your men move with variations of fakes and directions. In teaching your players a good maneuver, have your front man start toward the feeder to receive the pass. As the defense commits to pick off the pass, your player can cut off his lead foot and drive toward the basket. When the center is clear, your man will be able to receive the pass and go all the way. In doing this your team's action forces the defense to play more conservatively, which permits your offense to function normally. Blind screens set by the wing man on the pressing front defense will also enable the front man to break clear, creating another hazard and problem for the defense.

In summary, remember that a variation of screens must be used to free your team members for the necessary shots. Many times the collapsing defenses will reduce the effectiveness of these various maneuvers. Even though your efficiency might be reduced on a one-on-one with a collapsing defense, you can still force the defense to commit. When the defense has to do this, you can put pressure on any move the defense makes. With the movement off these variations and the possibilities present, your team can force the defense into unfavorable situations. As this occurs, your personnel must be able to recognize the opening and, with quick reaction and agility, capitalize on the defensive mistake.

These maneuvers cannot be perfected without long hours of practice. Attention to the possibilities must be stressed as the players are confronted with the various situations developed in scrimmage. This procedure will help your boys recognize the opportunities under game conditions. In any and all of these opportunities, maneuvers on the part of the individual team member must be blended and jelled into effective teamwork and organization for overall success.

Index

187

B